DATE DUE			

THEOLOGY AT THE END OF THE CENTURY

A Dialogue on
the Postmodern

with Thomas J. J. Altizer, Mark C. Taylor,
Charles E. Winquist and Robert P. Scharlemann

THEOLOGY AT THE END OF THE CENTURY

A Dialogue on the Postmodern

with Thomas J. J. Altizer,

Mark C. Taylor,

Charles E. Winquist

and Robert P. Scharlemann

Edited by
ROBERT P. SCHARLEMANN

University Press of Virginia

Charlottesville and London

THE UNIVERSITY PRESS OF VIRGINIA
Copyright © 1990 by the Rector and Visitors
of the University of Virginia

First Published 1990

Library of Congress Cataloging-in-Publication Data

Theology at the end of the century : a dialogue on the postmodern /
with Thomas J. J. Altizer . . . [et al.] ; edited by Robert P.
Scharlemann.
   p. cm. — (Studies in religion and culture)
  Papers presented at a symposium held at the University of
Virginia in 1988.
  ISBN 0-8139-1246-6
  1. Theology—20th century—Congresses. 2. Deconstruction—
Congresses. I. Altizer, Thomas J. J. II. Scharlemann, Robert P.
III. Series: Studies in religion and culture (Charlottesville, Va.)
BT28.T457   1990
230'.0904—dc20   89-49021
                                              CIP

Printed in the United States of America

CONTENTS

THEOLOGY AT THE
END OF THE CENTURY
A Dialogue on
the Postmodern
with Thomas J. J. Altizer, Mark C. Taylor,
Charles E. Winquist and Robert P. Scharlemann

ROBERT P. SCHARLEMANN

1

INTRODUCTION

THE ESSAYS in this volume have the nature of a symposium on the importance of the postmodern and for theological thought. Any dialogue on the postmodern, quite apart from the question of its pertinence to theology, faces difficulties. Most immediately it must deal with the indefiniteness of the concept of the postmodern. One does not have to read long or widely in the literature to become aware of the fluidity of the concept. Since that is the case, an effort must be made to provide an initial outline of the phenomenon under discussion. It will be easiest to do this by sketching some of its features. These will be intended to set off the concept of the postmodern from that of the modern. The features are intended to provide a broad description, not confined to one variety of the postmodern, such as poststructuralism in relation to structuralism or deconstruction in relation to ontotheology. It does seem possible to identify some features that characterize the postmodern as such. It might be objected that the effort to do this amounts to something still modern or metaphysical. That, however, is not necessarily the case. It is certainly possible to sketch features of a phenomenon, or to say what something is, without implying that these features are metaphysical essentials. Moreover, if we are using words in such a way as to suggest that they have a definite application, then we have some obligation to say what the words that we use mean in the context of our usage.

With that in mind, we can identify several distinguishing features of the postmodern in its significance for theological thinking. One of those features, frequently cited in the literature, is a questioning of the transparency of the self, or a challenge to the notion that the self which is conscious of itself is also fully transparent to itself, clear about the nature of its actions, motivations, thoughts, and feelings. In opposition to this understanding is the notion of the self which arises out of a psychoanalytical, if not specifically Freudian, dimension of the unconscious. A recognition of the unconscious is an acknowledgment that the self of our self-consciousness is not capable of making fully present to itself the contents of consciousness. The I of "I think" cannot play the role of providing the basis for a grasp and mastering of the world if there is a dimension of consciousness that remains inaccessible to reflection and eludes direct awareness. This idea itself is, admittedly, of an origin earlier than Freud. There is a version of it in the conception of mythology as a necessary process that Schelling developed in his philosophy of mythology and revelation. Nonetheless, it is Freud to whom we owe the by now general acknowledgment of this feature of the human self. We cannot appeal simply to a Cartesian understanding of the self in its full self-transparency in order to understand the structure or dynamics of selfhood. This is part of what Winquist in his essay refers to as the subversion of the understanding of the self. If, according to a Cartesian understanding, the recognition of the I-ness of the self in the thinking of "I am" makes the reality of the being of the self intelligible, then the postmodern view is that the being of the self—the "I am"—is what makes the "I think" unintelligible or obscure. Far from its being the case that the thought of the I clarifies the being of the self, the being of the I, which is expressed in the "I am," makes obscure or unintelligible the thought of the self as formulated in "I think." Theological thought cannot, then, seek to clarify the conception or the reality or the mystical beyond (ἐπέκεινα) of deity by reference to the clarity of the self in self-consciousness. Self-reflection does not clarify the meaning of being; rather, the being of things makes obscure the apparent clarity of reflection.

What is true of the Cartesian notion of the full transparency of the self to itself in thinking may also be true of the Kantian notion of the apperception of the transcendental ego. If we take the term *transcendental* to refer, as it does in Kant, to what is the condition of the possibility of actual knowledge or experience, then the transcendental ego, as the apperceived unity of experience, is a condition of the possibility of experience but is not itself an object of experience. We do not perceive this self in the way that we perceive objects such as stones, trees, flowers, and animals. Rather, we "apperceive" the self "purely." That is to say, along with our perception of empirical things we also spontaneously (not as the result of impressions on us) perceive the unity of the consciousness to whom the perception of things belongs.[1] To what extent the postmodern also involves an overturning of this Kantian notion of pure apperception or of the transcendental is not entirely clear. What is clear, however, in the postmodern conception of the subject is that there is no uniform or universal structure of the self that constitutes a transcendental ego and that there is always an element of the "not-mine" as well as of the "mine" in the totality of perceptions. This is to say not merely that there is cultural conditioning in all rational ideas and empirical perceptions but also that the linguistic effect upon ideas and perceptions is always more than is suggested by the notion of language as the bearer of concepts and of communication. We cannot define a structure of subjectivity, or even the idea of the pure I, independently of the linguistic milieu in which the words *I* and *self* or their counterparts in other languages appear, nor can we draw the not-I of the unconscious into consciousness by reflection alone. Thus, even though the concept of a transcendental ego might be the formulation of a condition of the possibility of experiences in the context of a Kantian philosophy, it is neither universally apperceivable nor necessarily transferable to the thought and experience that takes place in the medium of languages or linguistic traditions other than those of metaphysical thought. A simple formulation of this point is to say that subjectivity is pluralistic rather than universal. Each of us as a subject is a unique perspectival point of view and origin of action, in that each of us sees and thinks and feels from a point in time and space which cannot be exchanged with any other one and which therefore is unique. But, even beyond the perspectival differences, there is the difference of such a kind as to make impossible the reduction of a "thou" to another "I." The subjectivity of another subject is not only the same as my subjectivity, though differently located, but is also other than my own subjectivity.

These two characteristics—that the self is not transparent to itself because consciousness has no direct access to the realm of the unconscious and that there is an irreducible duality in the structure of subjectivity which makes the self pluralistic rather than universal in character—mark one feature of postmodern thought. A second feature is related to the Nietzschean declara-

tion of the death of God. It was probably Heidegger's studies of
Nietzsche, appearing in the years after *Sein und Zeit*, that drew
this distinctive connection between the themes of the death of
God and the end of metaphyics.[2] It is postmodern in the sense
that it too reflects a break with a form of thought in which the
ideas of the self, the world, and God are the purely rational and
intelligible ideas. We may recall that in Kant's philosophy, the self
in its freedom, the world in its totality, and God as absolute were
the three ideas constituting the metaphysical realm. Kant did not
question whether these ideas were intelligible; he questioned
only whether the realm indicated by them can be known at all—
whether, therefore, metaphysical knowledge is possible. And he
gave in the main a negative answer, at least insofar as theoretical
reason is concerned. Since there is no empirical reality of which
we can say, "That is the I" or "That is the world" or "That is
God," there can be no theoretical *knowledge* connected with
these ideas. Although Kant's questioning of metaphysics, in his
asking how metaphysics can be possible as knowledge, opens into
the direction of the postmodern, it is not yet the same as the
postmodern view of the end of metaphysics. This view is defined
more by Nietzsche and Heidegger than it is by Kant, and it is concerned with the association between being and God, and between
being and entities, that appears in the Western theological and
ontological tradition. Metaphysical thought, as Pöggeler put it,
"thinks that it can refer every entity to an ultimate ground." But
in doing so "man . . . places himself outside his own essence
[*Wesen*], to which there belongs the historical and uncontrollable
future"; and then "nature, which inexhaustibly goes out of and
back into its fullness, becomes an object of representation and a
mere state of affairs that is there for the ordering, and man becomes as Nietzsche puts it, the 'murderer of God': the godly is not
allowed its godliness if it is placed before man and for man as constantly present and thus available."[3]

In this way the Nietzschean declaration of the death of God signals a transition to the postmodern. Among the three contributors to the present symposium, it is, of course, Thomas Altizer
who has made this theme central to his theology. There, is, however, a variation on the theme that can be identified as a third feature of what is meant by the postmodern. This third feature is the
more specifically Hegelian understanding of the death of God.
What distinguishes Hegel's treatment from the earlier discussions of the death of God in theology is his incorporation of it

into a philosophical theology of world history itself. In Hegel the death of God is understood not only in the context of religious piety, as it had been earlier, but in the context of a philosophy of history. He was the first to incorporate this theme into a universal history by elevating the Christian imagery to philosophical significance. The change is indicated by the contrast between the theme of the death of God when it appears in the second stanza of Johann Rist's Good Friday hymn ("O Traurigkeit, O Herzeleid," 1641)—a hymn to which Hegel refers—and when it appears in the Hegelian philosophy of absolute spirit. In the context of the Good Friday hymn, the theme is an expression of Christian piety. It involves a recollection of the impact upon Jesus' disciples of the death of the one who, for them, had been the promised Messiah. It refers to that momentary loss of a world and a God on the part of those disciples out of whose experience the Christian church arose. It has the intensity of religious experience. The religious intensity is tranformed by Hegel into a moment of world history as the point at which spirit is most estranged from itself. Indeed, one of Hegel's stated intentions in his philosophy of history was to show how the providence of God, which theology only asserted as an object of faith, really is worked out in history.[4]

A fourth feature of the postmodern is indicated in the subtitle, *From Principles to Anarchy*, which Reiner Schürmann uses for his book *Heidegger on Being and Acting*.[5] If it is true that there is no such thing as a fully self-transparent ego, which can serve as the foundation for the theoretical and practical mastery of the world, then the loss of first principle means also that there is no such thing as a primary reality from which all other realities can be derived. There is then no absolute basis either in the subject or in the object of thought. That there is no absolute first in this sense is already brought out in Kant's analysis of the dialectic of the three ideas of pure reason. Each of these ideas is inherently dialectical because it seems to posit and then to deny the reality of what it names, and there is no synthesis of the positing and denying. The world, for example, both can and must be proved both to have and not to have a beginning in time and boundaries in space. The same is true of the existence of God and the immortality of the soul. The "metaphysical bent" reflected in the dialectic of these ideas is incurably human. Yet, in their own, illusory way, their *Schein*, the pure ideas are ideas *of* something and not just symptoms of a human disposition. The problem lies in finding out what the ideas are ideas of. It is in this dialectic that

Kant might be said to have introduced, without developing it, the possibility of a form of thinking no longer based upon a first principle or an absolute ground. Schelling's contention that at the bottom of final opposites is *Indifferenz* or *Ungrund* rather than identity takes a further step.[6] But it is only in Tillich's sketch of systematic theology which comes from the year 1913 and in his as yet unpublished essay "Rechtfertigung und Zweifel" from 1919 that we see an actual alternative to a metaphysics of first principles, or to what is now commonly called ontotheology.[7] It is an alternative connected with the notion of positive paradox. We need not here trace Tillich's development of this positive paradox. For, even though he may have been the first to lay hold of and to make visible the problem that appears later in the postmodern discussion of principles, the current discussion owes its terms less to Tillich than to the later Heidegger and to Derrida. This later discussion looks to "closure," rather than to "positive paradox," to avoid the self-annihilation that relativism and skepticism traditionally harbor. "Through language, theory, and text," Hilary Lawson concludes, "we close the openness that is the world. The closures we make provide our world. . . . We do not have different accounts of the same 'thing,' but different closures and different things."[8] Postmodern thought means, then, a recognition that just as there is no full transparency of the self to itself but a dispersal into concrete subjectivities, so there is no world as such but many "closures." Neither the transparency of the self (or subjectivity) nor the reality of the world (objectivity) nor the unity of the two as being or God can, therefore, serve as a final basis for thought and knowledge.

These can be seen as features outlining the phenomenon of the postmodern. Postmodern understanding or thought involves a definite view of the obscurity of the being of the self; it involves a definite view of the connection between the end of metaphysics based on a supreme being and the meaning of the death of God; it involves the transformation of the religious "Good Friday" into a world-historical event; and, finally, it involves a definite view of the possibility of replacing metaphysics of first principles with a form of thinking oriented to epochal arrangements. If the postmodern meant nothing more than the end of what Derrida refers to as logocentrism, it might be regarded as having theoretical or ontological, or even christological, significance but not theological significance. If, however, the ontological theme is simultaneously shown in its theological dimension, as is done when one speaks not only of the end of metaphysics but also of the death of the theistic God, then the characterization of the postmodern involves the kinds of features listed. There is, no doubt, basis enough for objecting even to this outline of the features. But the intention here is to provide an initial configuration of the object under discussion in these essays rather than to give a definitive account. If the end of the twentieth century is called postmodern, this is not meant to say that everything which appears in this period has these characteristics. For, although it may be true that such intellectual or spiritual phenomena as the postmodern can appear only at a certain stage of historical development, it is not true that the features appear in all aspects of what is chronologically contemporaneous. The postmodern should be treated as a distinctive, but not necessarily encompassing, contemporary phenomenon and as a phenomenon that calls for theological understanding.

A Theology of Culture

To speak of a theological understanding of the postmodern is to enter the context of what Tillich identified as cultural theology, or theology of culture. The idea that there can be a theology, indeed, that there is a theology, which is not religious or ecclesiastical but cultural in origin, was first set forth in the present century by Tillich in the essay of 1919 which bore the title "On the Idea of a Theology of Culture." Tillich's contention was that culture itself has a dimension to it which is theological in character. If that is so, then it is possible to think of cultural theology as existing alongside ecclesiastical or religious theology. That there is an ecclesiastical or religious theology one need not deny. What is important is to recognize—and this was also Tillich's concern—that this is not the only form in which theology can exist. The other form is cultural theology, a theology immanent in cultural works themselves. Tillich's own concern with cultural theology was a specific one. He was interested in understanding the theological character of an era, the era in Europe that began after World War I. The interest was not focused upon individual works of culture themselves but upon the spirit revealed in them all and revealed especially in their styles. This specific interest can, however, be disconnected from the notion of cultural theology as such. If a theological interpretation of culture is possible at all, then it can be carried out both as an interpretation of particular

works and also as an interpretation of an epochal spirit. For in either case, the theological significance lies in recognizing that we
can read theology from cultural works themselves and not only in
theological or religious books. How is such a cultural theology related to ecclesiastical theology? Tillich's own answer to that
question still sounds right. Ideally, he thought, the two should be
united in the person of the theologian. For each kind of theology
has an attendant danger. Cultural theology runs the risk of being
carried away with the winds of the time. Ecclesiastical theology
runs the risk of being a sterile traditionalism. Because each has its
own risk, though the risks are different, each can serve as a correc-
tive of the other. Cultural theology can serve to decalcify or, if
need be, to alter the traditional formulations, and ecclesiastical
theology can provide a critical distance for evaluating cultural
theology. If cultural theology runs the risk of being a cultural
expression only, ecclesiastical theology runs the risk of being a
preservation of religious ideology, instead of a theology. Because
of the thematic focus, no conscious effort has been made to include that kind of reciprocity of the cultural and the ecclesiastical
in the present volume.

The Editor as Interrogator

In putting this set of essays together as a symposium, the editor
has played more than the customary editorial role. We wanted the
dynamics of a dialogue to appear, if possible, in the published
form of the essays. Practical difficulties involved in trying to carry
on a dialogue in written form prevent a full realization of dialogue. That is already indicated by the third-person form of address used among the participants in the discussion. But we have
adopted the device of having the editor serve as an interrogator
and interlocutor of the three other essayists, a role somewhere between those of advocate and critic. Thus, the editorial response to
the three essays contains questions that were sent to the other
participants for replies. The nature of the replies was left entirely
to them, as one would naturally expect to be done. The replies, in
turn, complete the published part of the dialogue. But it is our
hope that they do so in such a way as to draw readers on their own
into the discussion. The questions to the essayists were formulated with two purposes in view. One was to illuminate the intention behind particular questions by supplying a background for
them. The second purpose was to make it possible for readers who

are not familiar with the terrain of the discussion to follow, and also to gain some grasp of the significance of, the discussion.

With regard to the response and the replies, attention needs to be called to one matter of detail. In Mark Taylor's reply, there is a reference to asterisks appearing at the end of the editor's response. Readers will not find any such asterisks there. Hence, an explanation is in order. The typescript of the response as it was sent to the three contributors did, indeed, conclude with a line of five asterisks. Their purpose, not indicated to the other authors, was purely utilitarian: they were used as a device in converting the footnotes of the typescript to endnotes for the printer. The asterisks themselves did not survive the conversion. However, Taylor's comments on them seemed worth preserving. Thus, it was decided to leave out the asterisks, after they had fulfilled their utilitarian purpose, but at the same time to retain the references to them in Taylor's essay. If nothing else, this will serve as one, however insignificant, illustration of something's being present, as it were, by its absence.

As one might expect, the thematic focus of the three main essays varies. Charles Winquist takes as his point of departure the Nietzschean declaration of the death of God, which along with Freud's impact on the understanding of the self has determined much of the literature of the postmodern, but he does so with particular reference to the way it affects the use and understanding of language. One of his arguments is that it is not metaphor but metonym that holds the key to the theological questions at stake. This presents a different grasp upon theological language from the one with which Ricoeur in particular has made us familiar in recent years through his work on metaphor. Thus, whereas Ricoeur argues that theological meaning is connected with the new worlds that are opened up metaphorically out of the clash of meanings that appears in the literal sense of language, Winquist looks rather to constellations of metonyms that appear as an unassimilable element in discourse; they do not open up new worlds of a text but serve to "defamiliarize" the familiar worlds. It is this unassimilability, rather than the disclosure of other worlds, that provides the theological dimension in language.

Again, locating the theological issue in language, rather than in epistemology, leads Winquist to shift the terrain of theology from the framework of subjectivity and objectivity to the question of language and the otherness of language. If it was characteristic of modern thought to take the distinction between subjectivity and objectivity as final in the sense that everything is ultimately either subjective or objective and every form of being is a form of relating subjectivity to objectivity, then the postmodern is identified by its location in language and by the problems of the relation of language, or discourse, to what is other than language.

There is a hermeneutical consequence of this shift as well, one that Winquist draws from Lacan's interpretation of the way Freud altered the modern concept of the subject. The effect is expressed in the idea that, contrary to nineteenth-century idealism, the self that objectifies itself in its own images also alienates itself in the process and makes itself unrecognizable to itself. Related to this is the change effected by Foucault in the Cartesian understanding of the "I think" and the "I am": it is not that the thinking of the self makes the being of the real intelligible but that the being of the self makes the real obscure to thinking.

The most direct theological significance of these changes in seen in the way theological texts are themselves to be read theologically. Winquist uses the theology of the death of God as a case in point. If this is read as an expression of the rise of secularity, or if, in other words, death-of-God theology is read as an expression or assertion of modern secularity, its theological meaning is missed. For the theological theme of the death of God is a theological counterreading—a reading against theological totalization—that belongs to theological discourse itself. The affinity between this understanding of theological discourse and Tillich's concept of the theological paradox makes it natural for Winquist to conclude his essay by an examination of how this double movement appears in the three basic doctrines of Tillich's systematic theology.

Mark Taylor's essay is in part a theological analysis of specific works of culture and in part an interpretation of the meaning of the end. Taylor makes use of certain contemporary paintings in order to read through them to an understanding of the contemporary situation. The reading has to do with the concepts of total presence and of nothing and their relation to the end of theology, where "end of theology" means a way of thinking of the end. In Yves Klein's paintings of monochromatic blue, on canvases without frames, Taylor sees the end that is the striving of painters as well as theologians, the ecstatic union with the all, in which the difference between exterior and interior is erased. The Messianic dimension in Klein's person and work suggests that there is here an effort to draw others into that same one-and-all.

A second painter to whom Taylor looks is Lucio Fontana. Fontana's cuts on monochromatic canvases show something differ-

ent. What is portrayed in his painting is not total presence but
rather the task that Taylor sees as the task at the end of theology—to think ending a/theologically, that is, as the neither-nor
and both-and that is beyond both the "being" and the "God" of
ontotheology. The nothing beyond the all must be thought by
some means other than the ways offered by ontotheology. But
doing so, Taylor argues, will also require seeing the end not as
apocalypse but as disaster. With this, he is led into a discussion
of Western consciousness as it appears in Altizer's *History as
Apocalypse.* This consciousness reaches its completion in Hegel's
philosophy of absolute spirit. Thus, Taylor continues by a discussion of that Hegelian self-consciousness and follows by drawing a
contrast between Hegel and Samuel Beckett, whose *The Unnamable* is interpreted as dismantling Hegel's system. In the two
figures, Hegel and Beckett, one can see the difference, as Taylor
indicates, between the idealistic and the contemporary conceptions of the self and its relation to the other. According to Hegel's
presentation of the appearing of absolute spirit, the self recognizes itself in its other and then returns to itself; the movement
of objectification and return is the movement through which
spirit comes to itself concretely as absolute spirit. By contrast, in
Beckett's *The Unnamable,* the other remains the unnamable.
That is to say, the self cannot recognize itself in any of its ob-
jectifications. These analyses lead into Taylor's formulation at
the end of his essay, namely, that the end is the disaster that is the
nonevent in which nothing happens, or the eternal delay of the
arrival of every present.

   In the third of the three essays, Altizer develops further the
theme of the death of God, with which his theology has always
been associated, in the form of a universal history that is at complete odds with the myth of eternal return. For the myth of eternal return, there is no difference between beginning and end; the
same always recurs. For the history that begins with the revelation of I Am, the beginning is unique, and the history is made up
of unique and irreplaceable events. This history begins, as does
language itself, with the breaking of the silence of the transcendent deity that occurs with the once-for-all self-naming of I Am;
and it ends with the equally singular silence of that name. That
event of revelation is unique, but it is also the event that makes
other events unique; it makes possible history in the sense of
events that are real not because they are everlasting but because
they pass away. Altizer bases his conception of the reality of
unique historical events precisely on the finality, or irreversi-

bility, of death. Hence there is a close interweaving throughout
his essay of the themes of death and reality and an emphasis
on the clear incompatibility between history so understood and
every form of primordial or archaic interpretations of the real,
every form of the myth of eternal return. The importance of biblical revelation, or the self-naming of I Am, lies in the fact that it is
the only real challenge to the eternal return. What occurs with
that revelation, however, is only gradually realized in the course
of history. In this, Altizer's theology of revelation is, like Hegel's
philosophy of religion, a theology of history. Transformations of
consciousness, revolutions, and the other marks of historical
movement, notably the violence connected with it, are made possible by, and are realizations of, what was begun with the revelation of the divine name. So much is this the case that one cannot
question the irreversibility or uniqueness of historical events
without questioning revelation itself. Historical turnings, revolutions, are rooted in the self-negation of the transcendent that is
contained in self-naming of I Am. What is true of history is also
true of the phenomenon of death. Revelation reverses the eternal
presence, it is the "actual death of eternal presence" or of deity as
transcendent. At the same time it ends every possibility residing
in the myth of an eternal return of the same.

In the rest of his essay, Altizer charts the historical realization
of the revelatory beginning by reference to some of the major
movements: apocalypticism and Augustinianism (the discovery
of the contingency of time as well as the contingency, or Faustian
energy, of the will) in the early centuries of the Christian church,
the Reformation conscience and the Satan of *Paradise Lost*, the
French Revolution, Nietzsche's nonarchaic conception of eternal
return, and modern apocalypticism—these events, among others,
are charted as events in which revelation is historically realized.
They reach their ending in the postmodern period, understood as
the "total realization of the Crucified God," when ending is occurring everywhere and filling everything with silence, "a silence
which is the silence of God."

NOTES

1. "I call [this representation of the "I think" which is given prior to all thought]
   pure apperception to distinguish it from empirical apperception, or, again,
   original apperception, because it is that self-consciousness which, while gen-

erating the representation 'I think' (a representation which must be capable of accompanying all other representations, and which in all consciousness is one and the same), cannot itself be accompanied by any further perception. The unity of this apperception I likewise call the *transcendental* unity of self-consciousness, in order to indicate the possibility of an *a priori* knowledge arising from it. . . . As *my* representations . . . [the manifold representations] must conform to the condition under which alone they *can* stand together in one universal self-consciousness, because otherwise they would not all without exception belong to me" (Kant, *Critique of Pure Reason*, B132–133).

2. See Otto Pöggeler, *Der Denkweg Martin Heideggers* (Pfullingen: Neske, 1963, 1983), pp. 104–42. It is noteworthy that Rudolf Otto discussed the "rational schema" of the wrath of God but not of the death of God in his book *Das Heilige* of 1917.

3. Otto Pöggeler, *Der Denkweg Martin Heideggers*, p. 137. The passage continues: "Metaphysics distorts entities and their being by thinking them. Its greatness is that it tries to think of entities in their being and opens the thinking of being in the direction of a subsistent divine. Its error [*Verfehlung*] lies in its not asking about the truth of being but, instead, taking being, in a manner not further thought through, as constant presence, so that being takes on the character of the disposable, and the thought that looks for grounds (or reasons) becomes a control over the grounds and the ultimate ground" (pp. 137–38).

4. On the significance of the theme of the death of God for Hegel, and the materials pertaining to Hegel's exposition of the theme, see Eberhard Jüngel, *God as the Mystery of the World*, tr. Darrell L. Guder (Grand Rapids, Mich.: William B. Eerdmans, 1983), pp. 63–104.

5. Reiner Schürmann, *Heidegger on Being and Acting: From Principles to Anarchy* (Bloomington: Indiana Univ. Press, 1987). Hilary Lawson's *Reflexivity* (La Salle, Ill.: Open Court, 1985) is an admirably lucid exposition of Nietzsche, Heidegger, and Derrida on just this matter.

6. See F. W. J. Schelling, *Philosophische Untersuchungen über das Wesen der menschlichen Freiheit und die damit zusammenhängenden Gegenstände* (1809), in *Schriften von 1806–1813* (Darmstadt: Wissenschaftliche Buchgesellschaft, 1968), esp. pp. 351f.

7. Paul Tillich, "Systematische Theologie," in John Clayton, *The Concept of Correlation* (Berlin: de Gruyter, 1980), pp. 253–68. The typescript of Tillich's 1919 "Rechtfertigung und Zweifel" (which is not the same essay as the one bearing the same title but coming from 1924) is in the Tillich archives at the Divinity School of Harvard University.

8. Hilary Lawson, *Reflexivity*, p. 128. There is, of course, a problem latent in the apparent contradiction between referring to the many closures of "the world" and asserting that the different closures are not of the same thing but of different things. To work out that problem would, I think, require a notion like that of Tillich's positive paradox.

CHARLES E. WINQUIST

2

THE SILENCE OF *THE REAL*:

Theology at the End

of the Century

> Never in any previous civilization have the great meta-
> physical preoccupations, the fundamental questions of
> being and of the meaning of life, seemed so utterly re-
> mote and pointless.
>
> FREDERIC JAMESON

> Of what is great one must either be silent or speak with
> greatness. With greatness—that means cynically and
> with innocence.
>
> NIETZSCHE

[margin note: why?]

NIETZSCHE'S POSTHUMOUS voice at the beginning of the twentieth century is a challenge to any assessment of the condition and future of theology at the end of the twentieth century. When the great metaphysical preoccupations seem remote and pointless, it would appear that the choice articulated by Nietzsche has been a choice of silence that brings in its wake the silence of God and the silence of *the real*. The sense of an ending that has brought with it a silence is not just an ending but it is also a turning. The end of the century is also the turn of the century. The ending brings us to silence, but a turning that acknowledges that ending can be turning into the silence that is a new speech and a new thinking.

It is the turn that interests me, a tropism toward the darkness of the unthought. It is a turn we find in Ray Hart's and David Miller's imaginal theologies, Mark Taylor's and Carl Raschke's deconstructive theologies, Jacques Derrida's and Julia Kristeva's deconstructive philosophies, Michel Foucault's genealogical histories, and Jacques Lacan's revision of psychoanalytic theory. Precursor figures are as diverse as Georges Bataille, Stéphane Mallarmé, Gertrude Stein, and Friedrich Hölderlin; but certainly three that stand out and have been labeled by Paul Ricoeur as masters of a hermeneutics of suspicion are Freud, Nietzsche, and Marx. What does it mean to think in this tradition?

Understanding the possibilitites for theological thinking at the end and turn of the twentieth century is in large measure an accounting for the subversion of Enlightenment and modernist understandings of the self by the sustained critique of subjectivity in Marxist, Nietzschean, and Freudian traditions of thought since the nineteenth century. The legacy of suspicion from the nineteenth century has contributed to an epistemic shift that has significantly altered the rules of discursive formation and practice so that the definitions and tasks of fundamental, systematic, and practical theology must be rethought.

To think after Freud, Nietzsche, and Marx and to think in their tradition of suspicion is a characteristic of what has come to be called postmodernism. This is not so much a historical location or period but a way of thinking. It is a thinking in a certain way that I want to suggest is governed more by metonymical constellations than by a metaphorical constitution. It is a textual production that resembles more the work of a *bricoleur* than an archaeologist. What I am suggesting is that language has coagulated around figures of discourse in conceptual formations in ways that have problematized traditional understandings of the tasks of epistemology and, correlatively, foundational theology. In particular it is the concept of the self and what was thought to be a self-evident subjectivity that have themselves become subject to interrogations so that they are no longer a referential ground for intelligibility.

Historical formations, positivities, and empiricities conflict with one another and make experience incommensurable with any unified subtext of meaning when examined in the force of the traditions of Marx, Nietzsche, and Freud. That is, in the force of criticism, what we one time thought to be self-evident grounds for thinking can in new configurations of discourse appear to be secondary formations. It is in fact theories of discursive formation following from what appear to be the dada of twentieth-century cultural achievements and the convolutions of modern history that have radicalized the readings of Marx, Nietzsche, and Freud that take us not to the roots but to an uprooting of rational meaning. The vertical fantasy of digging down for deeper meanings is constantly subverted and converted into a horizontal display of multiplicities and arrangements of increasing complexification. It is the pressure of the display of the multiplicities that denies the privileging of logocentricism and with it the positive and negative legacies of the ontotheological tradition. This includes the Western humanism of which this tradition was its host.

Even without a sophisticated and radical rereading of the hermeneutics of suspicion, the shifts of sensitivity and the visibilities that fill our experiences mark a semiotic turn in understanding that forces attentiveness to the productions of discourse. For example, whenever we think about what is real and important we are thinking at an intersection of psychological and religious discourses and generally within a tropics of discourse. There is an obvious nonliterality to the intersubjective talk of intimacy, love, and eroticism that would analogously apply to talk of ultimacy if it were to find a place in our secular culture. When I call my love "pumpkin," I am not using words literally. When I call ultimate reality "God," I am not using words literally. And it is also clear that what is sought is not a metaphorical likeness so much as an interruption of the discourse, a defamiliarization that makes this talk not ordinary talk. Placing a "pumpkin" or a "God" in the discourse alters the general economy of the discourse. The play of signifiers shifts its meaning with the metonymic troping of the discourse without changing any of the other words. Metonymy alters the differential play or intratextual referencing. The more powerful the trope, the more significant is the alteration of the economy of the discourse.

Examples of pumpkins and other figurations of intimacy may appear too silly or obvious when we are talking about a *numinosum* in extreme discourses; but they illustrate a strategy in textual production that is not radically different from some postmodern strategies in psychological, theological, and philosophical text production. The copula *is* can be used for a simple juxtaposition of signifiers as well as for establishing a metaphorical likeness. The transgression of ordinary language by the introduction of an unassimilable trope alters the economy of the discourse without making a literal or metaphysical claim. One of the strange tropes, a catachresis, is the reification of what is adjectival in normal usage into a thing that can only be a thing when it is a signifier in a text. The adjectival noun resists assimilation into the differential play of other signifiers and yet changes the discourse because it means what other signifiers are not.

Examples of these reified adjectives in the histories of psychology, philosophy, and theology are easy to find. The true, the good, and the beautiful complement from classical philosophy the unconscious from depth psychologies and the real from Lacanian psychologies. These formulations instantiate a silence within the general economy of discourse. That is, although there are aggregations of language around these formulations, they are not resolved by or dissolved into the surrounding language. One of the most explicit expressions of an unassimilable trope is in Lacan's reading of Freud, where there is a profound silence of the real. The real is not a metaphor because that would give it voice. This real is a metonym that changes other voices. The difference may seem strained or too subtle, but I think we can locate the importance for theology of these formulations if we further attend to Lacan's notion of the order of the real.

A turn to Jacques Lacan is a return to Freud and most importantly a return to what is unassimilable in Freud. It is Lacan's understanding of the subversion of the subject in Freud that has severe implications for theories of theological discourse and is an exemplary radical rereading of the hermeneutics of suspicion that now characterizes the turn that is also the end of the century. The move in Lacan is a move behind the adaptive strategies of Americanized ego-psychologies to originary wounds were the "it" of the unconscious is marked. In fact, in the many radical rereadings of the hermeneutics of suspicion there are many "its" that mark resistance to assimilation in strategies of hermeneutical restoration of the ontotheological tradition.

What we first notice when we narrow our focus by turning to Lacan and the secondary literature about the work and life of Lacan is that everyone has trouble reading Lacan. Muller and Richardson "call Lacan's writings a rebus. . . . Lacan not only explicates the unconscious but strives to imitate it."[1] We have no simple understanding of "Who is speaking?" when we read Lacan. We do not simply interrogate the text but we are interrogated by the text. This belongs to style. Lacan is teaching style. Jane Gallop suggests that Lacan's *Ecrits* are writerly texts "written not to be read."[2] The reader is implicated in a perpetual struggle of production. It is not a benign *agon*. The rebus is not a parlor game puzzle that is to be undone or put together. In reading Lacan we assume our inevitable castration in language.[3] Lacan's style is "the man to whom one addresses oneself," and as Gallop suggests, "the violence of Lacan's style is its capacity to make the reader feel nonidentical with herself as a reader . . . to make the reader feel inadequate to her role as 'the man to whom Lacan addresses himself,' that is, inadequate to Lacan's style."[4]

Lacan develops a style of analytical discourse that fixates a concept of the subversion of the subject that is at the same time an oxymoronic requirement for slippage in speech and writing leaving cuts, gaps, and spaces on the recording surface of experience. Reading Lacan is a lesson in Lacanian reading. A Lacanian reading is not a search for hidden significations but is an insistence on the letter of the text in the specific dialectic of text production. It would be a shallow misreading of Lacan to begin to search for hidden symbolic meanings in a literary text or for specific Lacanian concepts in a theological text. The real loss in a theological assimilation of Lacanian concepts would be the loss of the loss we experience in Lacanian discourse. When theological concepts are used to mirror rather than interrogate reality, the unrestricted scope of these concepts can transumptively relocate figurations of lack on a surface that seems to fill in the lack. For example, Lacan's formula for atheism, "God is unconscious," can be psychologically tamed if it is relocated from the Freudian unassimilable "it" into a confident discourse of theological consciousness-raising. Here, there would be a falling back on a specular figure of wholeness so that when the "it" of the unconscious God is remarked in symbolic discourse, it has been or could have been transposed into a different discursive situation that is not Lacanian. This possible scenario is better understood by examining Lacan's notions of orders of the imaginary, symbolic, and real and their relationships to the mirror stage.

Sometime in that interval of infancy between six and eighteen months, the child is able to recognize its own image in a mirror. The mirror stage is an identification and marks a transformation of the subject when the subject assumes an image. As Lacan says, "The *I* is precipitated in a primordial form."[5] A substitution occurs. The love of the image of the whole body is substituted for the autoerotic relationship to the partial objects of the fragmented body. The subject is separated from the primacy of perception of the fragmented body in the reflection of the primordial image of the whole body. The mirror image can be thought of as a referential fantasy, or imago, for a transcendental unity of apperception that is outside of the subject. This unification and totalization of form is virtual and alienated. The mirror image cannot be touched. Only the mirror can be touched. The image can be indexed only on an imaginary register. The mirror image is the reflection of a projection and as such is the privileged experience of structuring projections. The subject transcends and loses the molecular multiplicity of the subject. There is an imaginary mastery in the naming and idealistic unification of the image. The mirror is a surface and the image can be unified and total and have no depth. The surface of the mirror is a recording surface that lacks depth, lacks organs, lacks being.

It is in the mirror stage that the subject is reified as an image outside of intersubjective structures that are themselves a play of differences. Lacan's order of the imaginary becomes a realm where the play of differences is covered over by mirroring.[6] This appears to be a heuristic qualification to help explain how a tendency toward idealization can have empirical credibility. As Gallop says, "Lacan's writings contain an implicit ethical imperative to break the mirror, an imperative to disrupt the imaginary in order to reach the symbolic."[7] She goes on to suggest that the symbolic can only be reached as a tear in the fabric of the imaginary.[8] The move to the symbolic register is through the imaginary. When the imaginary is understood to be imaginary and not an empirical refuge, it is then located in a discursive situation that is intersubjective and differential. The imaginary experience is linked to the symbolic order as soon as it is given over to discourse. What is imaginary has voice in the symbolic order if it is to be anything other than a mute repetition of its scene of origination.

The identification of the imaginary order with the mirror stage and the accession to the symbolic can be understood as a strategy for differentiating language and symbolic discourse from a mimetic function. The goal of thinking is not an adaptation to the order of the real because the domain of the real is outside of the representation of the subject be it through the imaginary ego or through the representational play of the symbolic. The truth of the subject is found in the locus of the Other.

This claim only makes sense if we see how Lacan understands differential play in the symbolic order. It is here that we also see the originality of Lacan's use of linguistics to articulate his return to what is unassimilable in Freud. Lacan accepts the Saussurian distinction between the signifier and the signified. Meaning is made determinate in the interrelationship and play of differences between signifiers. The signified is itself in a web of signification that is always a play of signifiers. Unlike Saussure, Lacan emphasizes the bar separating the signifiers from the signified in the Saussurian algorithm. The circle or ellipse that embraces and unifies the Saussurian algorithmic expression of the barred relationship between signifier and signified is erased. The signified is absent in the present play of signifiers. There is no mimetic reference to the real. The bar is an aporia. Identity is in difference. The symbolic order is the possibility for deferral and difference. This is what it means to represent an identity.

This means that the Lacanian algorithm is a formula of separateness that does not admit of a reciprocity between the signifiers and the signified. This has a remarkable implication for the representation of the Freudian unconscious. "The unconscious is structured like a language."[9] We are never conscious of the unconscious as unconscious. It can only be known in an overdeterminate structure of language manifested symptomatically. The unconscious must be structured like a language, a play of signifiers, to have the referential motility that characterizes its formations. This is in Freud's language a consideration of representability. Lacan says that the linguistic structure "assures us that there is, beneath the term 'unconscious' something definable, accessible and objectifiable."[10] This is not the Freudian unconscious, but it does designate that it is in the symbolic order that we will encounter the unconscious. It will be in the symbolic order that the written or spoken sentence will stumble. There will be gaps, and as Lacan understands Freud, "the discovery" is in these gaps.[11]

What is discovered is not what is present. What is discovered is an absence. Quoting from Lacan: "The reality of the unconscious . . . is not an ambiguity of facts, future knowledge that is already known not to be known, but lacuna, cut, rupture inscribed in a certain lack."[12] The unconscious is what is unthought in thinking. It is where the fabric of the text gapes. It is in the sensuality of the trace—in what appears through what disappears. We might say that Lacan's return to Freud is a return of the repressed. We are back to the "it" of the unconscious, and "it" is anticonceptual and thus unassimilable. It resides in a domain that is always other. Repression delineates a domain of otherness.

There is a possible trap in this language that could lead to a theological misreading of Lacan. When Lacan talks about a grand Other, there is a temptation to objectify the other and name it God. It is then too easy to fill in the gap that is the importance of otherness. Lacan is concerned about the subject. The other is an object of the interrogation of the subject—"Who is speaking?" The interrogation of the Other reveals a lack. The Other is barred as the subject is barred. There is an otherness that represents what the grand Other lacks. In the phenomenality of the representation of desire the lack is the petite other of partial objects— an anus, a nipple, feces, the gaze, the phoneme, the nothing.[13] These petite objects do not represent a whole; they are what escapes the subject. They are the lack in the grand Other. They are the lack in the Other that constitutes the subject as subject. The limit of the unconscious is the concept of the lack.[14] One cannot build positive sciences of psychology or theology on this notion of the Other—on this notion of the unconscious.

Lacan indirectly teaches theology that it will not be a phenomenology describing otherness. Such a theology would be a catalogue of partial objects marking a lack, a loss, and constituting a desire. A theology responsive to Lacan will be a theology of desire unless it delimits its own interrogative structure. That is, what we encounter in Lacan that is immediately relevant for a theory of theological discourse is that its speech will always speak a lack and that the domain of its discourse is barred so that the otherness of reality does not belong to description but to desire. Theology must develop strategies of desire in language. We have returned to the question of style, which is where we began our discussion of Lacan because to think Lacan is to think style.

What we need is an articulation of textual strategies that accept responsibility in their own reflexivity for the repression of otherness. These are textual strategies that do not compensate for loss by a fascination with the exotic but work through themselves toward the significance of otherness. Desire references what discourse is not but it—the extratextual reference—is only known discursively. The problematic of desire in language is to acknowledge extralinguistic reference and yet stay within an internal play of linguistic signification.

What Lacan has articulated in the rereading of Freud that brings us to strategies of desire is both the need for and repression of the *other* of language that now problematically occupies the once confident place of subject-object relations in the framework of understanding. It is this dismantling of the subject that is so important in assessing where we are in understanding the possibilities for theological thinking. Lacan signals an epistemic shift that is larger than psychoanalysis or any other single discipline. The dismantling of the subject is indexed in all of the human sciences in these closing and turning times of the twentieth century.

What has been broken in the dismantling and general displacement of the subject is the supposed unity of apperception. We do not have an intuitive experience of an "I," or subject, behind statements. On the surface of a text, which is our immediate experience of a text, statements are multiplicities. We cannot assume a silent unity behind the statements although we may observe regularities between and among statements. We can construct diagrams, grids, and other abstract machines on the surface of the text, which is a work of interpretation, and then reference these constructs as a subjectivity in the text. When this is a conscious operation, thinking is not haunted by a ghost in the machine but is identified with the machine.

That is, the subject experiences as it is experienced in its constructedness. The carrying this experience over from the realm of the imaginary into the realm of the symbolic is making conscious the differential play that is constitutive of subjectivity. The experience of the subject in the mirror of the imaginary realm can obscure the multiplicity of subjectivities in the unity and opacity of a single image. In the symbolic or semiotic realm, the dispersion of subjectivity in language "that dispossesses it while multiplying it within the space created by its absence" is a tensive construction that can give meaning to subjectivity, but it will never be a singular meaning.[15] It is much more obvious in the symbolic realm that subjectivity is derivative than it is in reflections of the imaginary. That is, displacement of the subject through dispersion is much more obvious in the symbolic realm.

This is one of the reasons for beginning a discussion of the present theological task with a discussion of Lacan. The problematic of the subject is implicated in the reading of Lacan because of his distinction between the imaginary and symbolic realms that does not allow for retreat behind the opacity of images in referencing subjectivity. He also continues to pressure the discourse by not identifying the real with either the imaginary or the symbolic. The differential play in the realm of the symbolic that constitutes the meanings of subjectivity and intelligibility and the quasi-transcendental rules that govern this discursive achievement do not at the same time constitute or exhaust the realm of the real.

The problematic of the subject in Lacan parallels Foucault's insight that "man, in the analytic of finitude, is a strange empirico-transcendental doublet, since he is a being such that knowledge will be attained in him of what renders all knowledge possible."[16] It might first appear that this is a return to the Cartesian cogito, but in both Lacan and Foucault the doubling in the cogito does not give sovereignty to the subject but instead problematizes it by embedding the "I think" in the otherness of what is not thought. The implication of the "I Am" in the "I think" is a displacement of subjectivity from a realm of pure thought into a nexus of relations and set of operations that do not themselves imply consciousness and if known to consciousness may be known only in their symptomatic presentation.

The "I think" is not an illumination of the "I Am"; but, instead, the "I Am" is a darkening of the density and complexity of the "I think" so that the "I think" of the cogito is a coassertion of the unthought. This unthought density of the human doublet has been part of the human enigma since the assertion of the cogito, but since the hermeneutics of suspicion in the nineteenth century it has insistently accompanied thought into the twentieth century. An analytic of finitude is now not credible unless it acknowledges forces of alienation, unconscious processes, the will to power, or other expressions of that which is other than pure reason.

In Foucault's language: "Man has not been able to describe himself as a configuration in the *episteme* without thought at the same time discovering both in itself and outside itself, at its borders yet also in its very warp and woof, an element of darkness, an apparently inert density in which it is embedded, an unthought which it contains entirely, yet in which it is also caught."[17] The further implication of this claim is that "discourse is not the majestic unfolding manifestation of a thinking, knowing, speaking subject, but, on the contrary, a totality, in which the dispersion of the subject and his discontinuity with himself may be determined."[18]

Both the self of the subject and the discourse of the subject are thought in such a way that the subject is implicated in what the subject is not. Subjectification is a process that goes outside the discourse of the self as is evidenced in the discontinuities of discourse. This going outside would be unintelligible if it were not

that the human subject is a "transcendental-empirico" doublet.
The outside is also an inside.

This claim is not at the same time a claim for a substantial self.
The constitution of the subject is a textual production that has
the peculiar characteristic of turning in on itself. Gilles Deleuze
describes this process in relation to the interaction of forces. "The
most general formula of the relation to oneself is the affect of self
by self, or folded force. Subjectivation is created by folding."[19]
This folding includes the materiality of the body, the bending of
lines of intersection of surrounding forces so that the outside has
an interiority. Inside and outside contract in a differential play of
contrasts constituting the meanings of both consciousness and
subjectivity without ceasing to be themselves. "These folds are
eminently variable, and moreover have different rhythms whose
variations constitute irreducible modes of subjectivation. They
operate 'beneath the codes and rules' of knowledge and power and
are apt to unfold and merge with them, but not without new fold-
ings being created in the process."[20] In this description the subject
is a derivation of the outside. The unity of apperception is a variable product of external multiplicities.

This means that there is a variable and heterological infrastructure for the folds of knowledge. There may be regularities across
diverse domains of discursive practices and the indexing of these
regularities gives us a general sense of knowledge with a thematic
stability but not a structural certainty. These regularities may
have a quasi-transcendental status. That is, they may be the product of a transcendental inquiry into the conditions that make
knowledge possible. But the status of transcendental inquiry is
interrogative and not descriptive.

The discovery of rules for the formation of discursive understanding is specific to an interrogation of a specific discourse and
these rules are not universal *a priori* forms of sensibility or categories of understanding. There is nothing about the specific fold
of transcendental interrogation that implies universal application. Its inside is always the folding of a specific outside. The conditions of possibility are material and historical. There is no
inside or outside that is a proper domain for a metadiscourse.
Metadiscourses are themselves folds implicated in both the in-
sides and outsides of specific discourses, implicated in the other
in and of language. Transcendental inquiry does not yield a foundation for discursive practices but it is a complication in the inscription of subjectivity in the formation of a new discourse.

That we do not have this foundation or even a meaning of subjectivity that is invariant across different domains of discourse alters the status of foundational theology as an inquiry from which
we could draw criteria for the evaluation of systematic theological formulations to a preliminary interrogation that problematizes theological text production in any of its specialties.
Foundational theology cannot establish itself as privileged in relationship to the other theological specialties because it too is fully
implicated in the formation of discourse of which it is but another fold. The subjectivity that it interrogates is its own production although the production is an operation within a nexus of
forces and already existing textual manifestations that are constitutive elements in the fold of interrogation.

In foundational theology there is no return to a point of reference that is criteriological for the further development of knowledge. There is no centering around a subject that can unify diverse
discourses. There is, however, the formation of a nomad subjectivity that is neither exclusively female or male, white or black,
east or west in its multiple manifestations but is, instead, socially
located in the specificity of its situation of origin. That is, transcendental interrogation is a subjectification of textual experience on a heterological base that is situation-specific. The logocentrism that is a subjective fold of the ontotheological tradition
is denied universal application in the formation of religious discourses. The possibilities for nomad subjectivity pressures discourses to convolute in further complications of the enigma of
the human doublet by revealing the constitutive function of
language and the quasi-transcendental status of rules for the
formation of discourse. Language usage itself has to be rethought
in terms of what is unthought in the production of multiple
subjectivities.

This does not mean that we can think what does not give itself
to thought or think outside of the folds of textuality. What it does
mean is that there are no epistemologically pure formal conditions for knowledge. What it does mean is "that the forms of human consciousness and the mechanisms of human psychology are
not timeless and everywhere essentially the same, but rather
situation specific and historically produced."[21] Nomad subjectivity is the product of specific and heterogeneous forces that are
known only in a differential folding that is nonidentical with the
situational nexus of forces that are the conditions of its possibility. There is no interpretive subject outside of this complex that

can work its will to exhaust or master the forces that constitute its appearance. The inscription of the subject is an enfolding so that it is never able to be an outside controlling agency. Nor is it an inside controlling agency independent of the outside since it is constituted as a fold of what is exterior and other than itself.

What we are here describing is thinking as an activity or practice that is fundamentally materialistic. There is a deep resonance with Karl Marx's first thesis on Feuerbach in which Marx is critiquing Feuerbach's materialism. "The chief defect of all hitherto existing materialism [that of Feuerbach included] is that the thing, reality, sensuousness, is conceived only in the form of the *object or of contemplation* but not as *sensuous human activity, practice,* not subjectively." [22] This sensuous human activity works with what is at hand. Its production is a bricolage that is manifest in the materiality of a text.

The loss of the single subject and the production of nomad subjectivities is incorrigible to the hermeneutic restoration of the ontotheological tradition. The alogic of rhetorical figurations materially privileges itself through insistent multiplication over patterns of theoretical unification. That is, discourse is pressured by its own production of subjectivities to subvert hegemonic unification in a single pattern of subjectivity whether that pattern be divine or an essential definition of the human. This decentering of subjectivity is an epistemic shift of major proportions.

In trying to understand the scope and importance of this shift, Mikhail Bakhtin describes the authentic environment of utterance as dialogized heteroglossia. He then says: "It is necessary that heteroglossia wash over a culture's awareness of itself and its language, penetrate to its core, relativize the primary language system underlying its ideology and literature and deprive it of its naive absence of conflict." [23] The one thing that the ontotheological tradition cannot do and still be itself is to relativize its primary language system.

For example, the commitment to first principles is set adrift by the heterological infrastructure of nomad subjectivities or Bakhtin's understanding of discourse in an environment of dialogized heteroglossia. This does not mean that one cannot be about the task of forming "first principles"; but it does mean that those principles are not going to function as first principles have been traditionally understood to function. They will have no privilege inside of language and no reality outside of language. They are a particular fold or specific turn of language and therefore function in the general tropology that we know as language. They, along with other philosophical and theological formulations, are figures of speech subject to rhetorical analysis.

Certain figurations will dominate a discourse by pressuring the differential play of textual and intertextual referencing in the complex of knowledge and power. Their assimilation into a discursive practice requires a more complex folding that alters the already existing economy of the discourse. Since what is known is already a mixture of force and figuration, a new folding in a sensuous operation displaying new differential intensities in the articulation of meaning. The authentication of meaning is not a process of reference but is a production that is self-authenticating through the intensities of its own achievement. Production includes processes of textual and intertextual referencing as elements of productivity, but these processes do not then stand independently of the production in judgment of its formative achievement. The power of the discourse resides in the complex of forces that are only visible in the multiplicity of folds that are differential contrasts between inside and outside held in conflictual tension only as the outside is folded inside. The forces are not the visibilities. It is the fold that is visible.

Whatever we know will be a surface. Every domain of discourse and knowledge will have folds and curvatures marking its surface specific to its achievements. Descriptive analysis of a discursive domain will be topographical, and transcendental analysis will be tropological. That is, we can describe the folds as visibilities in the surface manifestations of experience and also inquire into the formative turns or tropes that have variegated the surface. The assessment of the state of any discursive discipline is subject to this twofold analysis, and at the same time we always have to understand that the analysis is changing the surface and altering the practice it is analyzing. There is no frozen or stable surface, and there is no way of bracketing analysis so that it is not implicated in the formation, reformation, and deformation of the surfaces of understanding.

When we explicitly turn to an analysis and assessment of theology we must realize that this turn is itself a folding and that the theological use of language in both description and interrogation is tropological. We cannot turn to theology without fully implicating our inquiry in the heterological infrastructures of nomad subjectivities and at the same time the textual surfaces of the ontotheological tradition. The topographical and tropological analyses will conflict and tensively interact with each other. The task will not be unlike that described by Rodolphe Gasché in *The Tain of the Mirror*. "The deconstructive undoing of the *greatest totality*, the totality of ontotheology, faithfully repeats this totality in *its* totality while simultaneously making it tremble, making it *insecure* in its most assured evidences."[24]

Theology has traditionally been a discourse of extremities. Perhaps more than in any other discourse the formulation of basic concepts (Allah as Lord of the worlds, that than which nothing greater can be conceived, ultimate concern, the complete set of answers to the complete set of questions, the Brahman, absolute nothingness, the instantiation of a radical negativity, history as apocalypse) is a movement toward a totalization that when it turns on itself reveals those traits of discourse writ large that mark its heterological infrastructure. We can read any theology against the grain of its movement toward totalization and recover an agenda for theological thinking in our time. In this way theology can subvert itself and at the same time assert its importance as a radical discursive practice.

The agenda of radical theological thinking will not be identical with the agenda of traditional theology although it will make no less of a claim on thinking in the general economy of discursive practices. Setting the agenda among the various theological specialties has often been the task of foundational theology so that the interrogation and revaluation of concepts in foundational theology has implications for systematic and practical theology. In fact it is the accounting for the epistemic shift in foundational theology that suggests a reading against the grain of totalization in systematic theologies.

To explicate this point we could look at any of the fuller expressions of traditional theology and thereby better understand the transformation of the theological agenda in radical theology. I would suggest, however, that it is in the reading of theologies that are self-conscious of their functional specialties and self-conscious of their relationship to philosophy that we can most readily articulate or easily access the implications of the epistemic shift in foundational theology. Using this criterion, obvious candidates from the twentieth century for exemplary readings against the grain of totalization would be process theologies, existential theologies, and transcendental neoscholastic theologies. And among these theologies there is no single theology that is more explicitly aware of its indebtedness to the ontotheological tradition of nineteenth-century German idealism and general mortgage to the autonomous subject of Cartesianism than is the theology of Paul Tillich.

There is also a profound indebtedness in much contemporary theology to Paul Tillich's theology even when it is not explicitly acknowledged. It was his method of correlation that reinforced a tradition of making theology answerable to secular culture and opened the possibilities for a proliferation of secular theologies and conflicts of interpretations that have contributed to the interrogation of theological foundations. Reading Tillich against the grain of totalization is an extension of reading Tillich from the perspective of his own understanding of the Protestant principle.

Another important reason for choosing to look at Tillich in setting the agenda for theology is that in his later work he was clearly trying to assess the importance of the history of world religions for theology.[25] He addressed the concreteness and specificity of religions and recognized that the "concrete spirit" of religions abides in a tension between their particular manifestations and qualifications of ultimacy. That tension is marked on the surface of his own thought, and I think it marks an important heterological fold in his discourse that is consistent with his understanding of ultimate concern. It is his understanding of ultimate concern that pressures his discourse to wander outside of the containment of the Western ontotheological tradition and makes it even possible to ask about the importance of the history of world religions.

In his earlier systematic theological investigations it is his use of the concept of being and its possibly tensive relationship with the claims of an ultimate concern that surface in an interrogation of the discursive practices of foundational theology or in the encounter with non-Western traditions. In volume 2 of *Systematic Theology*, Tillich describes and summarizes the importance of introducing the concept of being into theology:

> When a doctrine of God is initiated by defining God as being-itself, the philosophical concept of being is introduced into systematic theology. This was so in the earliest period of Christian theology and has been so in the whole history of Christian thought. It appears in the present system in three places: in the doctrine of God, where God is called being as being or the ground and the power of being; in the doctrine of man, where the distinction is carried through between man's essential and his existential being; and, finally, in the doctrine of the Christ, where he is called the mani-

festation of the New Being, the actualization of which is the work
of the divine Spirit.[26]

The reader of Tillich can look at any of these three places to see
the implications of framing a systematic theology in the ontotheological tradition and then see what it means to deny that tradition its privilege. The first serious challenge to the privilege of
this tradition in Protestant theology in the twentieth century was
the restatement of Nietzsche's proclamation of the death of God.
    The force of this challenge, which should have led to a major
revision of the theological agenda, except in the ongoing work of
Altizer, was dissipated in a too easy accommodation with notions
of secularism and celebrations of the secular city. Perhaps we are
still in the situation of Nietzsche's madman who after proclaim-
ing the death of God said: "I have come too early . . . my time is
not yet. This tremendous event is still on its way, still wandering;
it has not yet reached the ears of men."[27]
    We are still not ready for the most explicit challenge to the
power of the ontotheological tradition, the challenge to the doctrine of God. When the great metaphysical preoccupations seem
"so utterly remote and pointless," a proclamation of this scale is
greeted with silence and condemned to a silent efficacy. But the
problematizing of the subject in the human sciences also is a serious challenge to the power of the ontotheological tradition and
it slips into our discourse like a Trojan horse. The subversive
power of constituted nomad subjectivities is very clear when they
undermine the distinction between essential and existential being
in what Tillich calls the "doctrine of man." The identification
of God with being-itself is systematically interwoven with the
understanding of fallen humanity and the meaning of human freedom. The deracination of any one of these concepts has implications for understanding the others.
    Tillich's understanding of freedom requires a unified subject. In
a discussion of Pelagian moral freedom and Manichaean tragic
destiny, he asserts: "Freedom is not the freedom of indetermi-
nacy. That would make every moral decision an accident, unrelated to the person who acts. But freedom is the possibility of a
total and centered act of the personality, an act in which all the
drives and influences which constitute the destiny of man are
brought into the centered unity of a decision."[28]
    The deconstruction of the subject that we examined in the

work of Lacan would in this context be a destruction of the self. Tillich even describes evil as the structure of self-destruction or the loss of the self. "Self-loss as the first and basic mark of evil is the loss of one's determining center. . . . Self-loss is the loss of one's determining center, the disintegration of the unity of the person."[29] The idiom for this description is psychological, but the explanatory structural frame is ontological.

The subject is an intentional agent that gives meaning to the concept of the self. Tillich describes the basic structure of finite being as a polarity of self and world. "Only man has a completely centered self and a structured universe to which he belongs and at which he is able to look at the same time."[30] There is a dismantling of the Tillichian self in the assertion that the truth of the subject is found in the locus of the Other. The force of this claim against the formulation of the Tillichian subject is somewhat obscured by Tillich's powerful descriptions of the self under the conditions of existential estrangement. That is, in these descriptions it appears that Tillich has a real grasp on the dispersion of subjectivity, but we have to remember that this is the description of a fallen human condition. The Tillichian self that is subverted by our reflections on Lacan is the self of essential being. This is not an unimportant distinction because it is the relationship between essential and existential being that is so deeply rooted in the ontotheological tradition.

"The transition from essence to existence is the original fact. It is not the first fact in a temporal sense or a fact beside or before others, but it is what gives validity to every fact. It is the actual in every fact."[31] We are not talking about the residue of an older tradition in Tillich's thinking that can be ignored. The transition from essence to existence is the scene of origination for an understanding of the human subject and definition of the self. The scene of the Fall may occupy a similar place in the analytic of finitude as Derrida's scene of writing, but its articulation leads to very different understanding of the human subject.

As Tillich notes: "The difficulty is that the state of essential being is not an actual stage of human development which can be known directly or indirectly. The essential nature of man is present in all stages of his development, although in existential distortion."[32] This essential nature has potentiality but not actuality. It has no place and it has no time. It is inaccessible in itself. In a metaphorics of the inaccessible Tillich refers to this essential being of the human as a state of dreaming innocence. What is the status of this state of dreaming innocence in theological discursive practices?

Since Tillich has not developed a critical theory of discursive formations, we are imposing a question on his systematic investigations that is shifting the discourse to a different register of intelligibility. The meaning of "dreaming innocence" is not referential in the specificities of place and time. It does not function in the same way as other concepts but anticipates an intelligibility that will be known only as it is other than itself in distortion through existential realization that is in place and time. The question is whether we can accord any originary status to "dreaming innocence" as an expression of essential being. Is the original fact the transition from essence to existence, or is the concept of essential being already in the imaginary and symbolic registers and secondary to a more original scene of folding?

On the level of phenomenological description we cannot talk of essential being. There is, however, a tension between the witness of estrangement and the witness of communities of faith to the New Being in Jesus as the Christ. "The appearance of the New Being under the conditions of existence, yet judging and conquering them, is the paradox of the Christian message."[33] Tillich says that this paradox is a new reality. This paradox can be marked in a phenomenological description, but it is not explained by it or contained within it. Tillich goes outside of phenomenology for an explanation, and the explanatory concepts that frame the descriptive tension are ontological.

The importance of claiming that the transition from essence to existence is the original fact is that it gives precedence to and justifies ontological explanation. It is the ontological framing of the discourse that gives the Fall universal applicability to descriptions of finite being rather than the force of the phenomenological description of estrangement. The ontological framework of explanation eases the conceptual tension between the witnesses to estrangement and the New Being in Jesus as the Christ. But the ontological framework entails an essential subject that is subverted by transcendental interrogations that generate nomad subjectivities.

Ontological explanation serves the paradox of the Christian witness in Tillich's theology, but that witness is not its foundation. Tillich formulates his ontological categories out of the context of a transcendental inquiry. It is the philosophical frame that is specifically embedded in the ontotheological tradition.

He defines philosophy in terms that are Kantian and transcendental even though the use of philosophy is ontological. "The question regarding the character of the general structures that make experience possible is always the same. It is *the* philosophical question."[34] Although these structures are defined as ontological and function as structures of reality as a whole, they are discovered and marked on an epistemological register through a critical analysis of experience. "Ontological concepts are a priori in the strict sense of the word."[35] In talking about finitude and explanatory categories, he claims that these categories are ontological but also says that "categories are the forms in which the mind grasps and shapes reality."[36]

There is a tension in these definitions. Subjective reason grasps and shapes reality, but it is reality as such that "is the structure which makes reality a whole and therefore a potential object of knowledge."[37] There is a conflicting primacy between epistemological and ontological claims concerning the formal manifestations of reality. This conflict suggests a transversal reflexivity that implicates the formation of epistemological and ontological concepts in each other. There is a folding in Tillich's own expression of this relationship. "Self-relatedness is implied in every experience. There is something that 'has and something that is 'had' and the two are one."[38]

In its grasping and shaping, subjective reason constructs ontological concepts; but "the truth of all ontological concepts is their power of expressing that which makes the subject-object structure possible. They constitute this structure; they are not controlled by it."[39] The subject constitutes the structure by which it is constituted. There is an undecidability about priorities in this formulation. The autonomy and priority of subjectivity are subverted by its own achievement, and the autonomy and priority of ontological structures are subverted by being an achievement of subjective reflection.

Transcendental interrogations as they are understood by Tillich traverse the domains of epistemology and ontology. In whatever domain we begin to question conditions of possibility we soon discover that the determinations of identity are in the other domain. There is no determinate standpoint that is not implicated in what is other than itself. There is no epistemological or ontological description or frame that is self-authenticating. There is incompleteness and indeterminateness in the discursive practices of these disciplines because they are not pure.

The absence of closure means that neither ontology nor epistemology can assert a universal privilege in the formation of other discursive practices. They are themselves heterological discourses that when viewed together may appear to approximate a totality; but there is also a sense in which they subvert each other by their individual claims to primacy. We do not have either in the language of ontology or in the language of epistemology universal formulations that can liberate thinking from bondage to the specific scenes of their origination because they are never complete in themselves and thereby free from those scenes. The claims to universality would require a transcendence of the heterological infrastructures in the formation of the discourses if they are to be a credible claim. The impurity of origination introduces an element of doubt.

The doubt raises the question as to where to locate the claims to universality that arise out of a specific and impure transcendental interrogation. The foundational categories of Tillich's theology are neither purely epistemological nor purely ontological. They, like many of Tillich's concepts, are on a boundary. I think that this is a very special boundary that can better be thought of as a frame. They constitute in their expression a materiality, spacing, thickness, and double-edged quality of a frame. The function of the frame is to make a contrast between the inside and the outside or between a figure and its ground. The double edges of a frame introduce an ambiguity in its functioning.

If we talk about framing a discourse, from the inside of that discourse the internal edge of the frame is the point of contrast between the figure and ground, inside and outside, so that the frame belongs to the ground or ourside. From the outside of a discourse the external edge of the frame is the point of contrast between the figure and ground, inside and outside, so that the materiality and structure of the frame appear to be internal to the specific figures of discourse.

If in the ontotheological tradition there is a subject of the transcendental unity of apperception that is delineated in the language of essential being and structures of essential being which in the analytic of finitude are grounded in the transcendental unity of apperception and which in combination frame a theological discourse, from the outside of the frame it would appear that this theological discourse is implicated in essential being without ever being explicitly ontological, and from the inside it would appear that this discourse is grounded in the structure of being without ever being explicitly ontological. There would always be a pressure on the discourse to become explicitly ontological because of the presence of an uncanny trace of the absence of being in the actual figures of theological discourse. The pressure would be toward closure in the totalization of the discourse.

The framing of a discourse does have specific location in the formation of the discourse. But because it is not part of the actual figures of discourse it seems to be no place and in no time. Its specificity is erased in the reciprocity of perspectives from outside and inside domains of discourse. This is the sleight of hand that occurs in shifting back and forth between ontological and epistemological interrogations. To read theology against the grain of totalization is to attend to the absences that reveal the presence of a frame and thereby denaturalize its effect on the discourse it frames.

Framing is part of the folding of discourses. The frame could only appear to isolate discourses. But discourses are instead always a heterological weaving so that the fabric of a discourse should have irregularities, seams, and tears as traces of alterity. This means that there should even be fissures in dominant theological figurations revealing lines of force or traces of alterity that witness to their heterological origins.

As we noted earlier, in all of the peregrinations of Tillich's theology, it is *being* that "remains the content, the mystery and eternal *aporia* of thinking."[40] When the frame of theological discourse is the ontotheological tradition, we have some understanding of why being is both a content and mystery of thinking. It does not function as a descriptor in the discourse except to locate the aporia of thinking.

It is in his doctrine of God that Tillich inserts the concept of being-itself without any qualifications. "The statement that God is being-itself is a nonsymbolic statement. It does not point beyond itself. It means what it says directly and properly."[41] What is interesting is that this statement in itself without any reference beyond itself doesn't mean anything. Tillich himself also says that "after this has been said, nothing else can be said about God as God which is not symbolic."[42] The talk of God as being-itself is denied entry into the differential play of discursive formations. As soon as we move to the symbolic register, talk of God as God is silenced.

In the symbolic register the naming of the "living God" transgresses the concept of God as a pure identity of being as being.

Tillich says that "God is a symbol for God."[43] He talks of the God above God and of God as the ground of being.

In all of these formulations the concept of God ceases to be identical with itself—identical with being-itself. The nonsymbolic statement that "God is being-itself" can, of course, only reside in the symbolic register. It is a formulation that, as it is stated, cannot be assimilated into a differential play and in this sense is a violation of the symbolic register.

It would appear that under the pressure of the unassimilable concept of God as being-itself, Tillich has formulated a number of nonconceptual concepts that then populate his theological discourse. These nonconceptual concepts do not function to establish identities. Their presence in a discourse denies privilege to the copula of being. Thus, it might first appear that the "is" of "being" functions metaphorically following patterns of analogy and establishing likenesses between dissimilars. This solution is too easy because although it would allow for the continuation of God-talk, the God that is talked about would not be God as God or function as mystery and aporia in violation of the homogeneity of the symbolic order.

Populating a discourse with nonconceptual concepts is a troping of the discourse, but the dominant trope in this formation is not metaphor. There is a radically disjunctive and wholly other claim on a discourse in the formulation of God as being-itself. In fact, all of the derivative dominant God concepts in Tillich's discourse function so radically that their juxtaposition in discourse is metonymical rather than properly metaphorical. They do not establish likenesses between dissimilars as approximations of identity. The use of *is* in the symbols of God established nonidentities. This is an oxymoronic state of affairs when Tillich also claims that "God is being-itself."

What I am suggesting is that since Tillich's own radical formulations for God work against the nonsymbolic or metaphorical privileging of the *is* in the establishment or approximation of identities, his use of the *is* is more closely associated in practice with forcing a metonymical alignment of the ordinary with formulations and qualifications of ultimate concern.

The nonsymbolic use of the *is* is an aporia that allows theology to go nowhere, and the metaphorical *is* is a diminution of the force of figurations of ultimacy in the formations of discourses. A metonymical use of *is* marks a space of juxtaposition for nonconceptual concepts or other figurations of ultimacy. These forced juxtapositions would pressure the discourse and alter its general economy. The discourse would then be implicated in ultimacy manifested through transformations of the ordinary. The discourse would then meet Tillich's first formal criterion for theology. "The object of theology is what concerns us ultimately. Only those propositions are theological which deal with their object insofar as it can become a matter of ultimate concern for us."[44] Even if the discourse is not ontological it can be theological through strategies of metonymical pressuring. This means that even when we read Tillich against the grain of totalizing movements in his theology, it is still possible to stay within the theological domain.

A new agenda for theology that is both in and at the end of the twentieth century surfaces in this reading of Tillich that is not just a modification of Tillich. When Tillich's exemplary investment in the ontotheological tradition is turned on itself we have a fairly clear reading of how the theological agenda must be revised if we are to account for both the proliferation of nomad subjectivities and the desire for totalization in the closure of the symbolic order.

First, the dismantling of the centered and unified subject means that theological subjectivity is constituted as it is written into and dispersed throughout the theological text. Foundational theology is not an inquiry that is outside of the discursive practices of theology but is an interrogation of those practices. Its principles are the quasi-transcendental rules for the formation of discourses and disclose not on ontological structure to subjectivity but a heterological infrastructure for multiple subjectivities.

Second, the deconstruction of constituted subjectivities denaturalizes the ontotheological frame of theological discourse. The frame is a materialistic fold in a specific nexus of forces relative to its social and intellectual location. The frame would not be the ontotheological tradition if the fold of consciousness were not located in a Western intellectual, social, and political context. But even in this tradition what is inside the frame is implicated in the other of what was outside and is now nonidentical with itself because of the fold. There is always an excess that has an undecidable quality.

Third, the traces of the other in the formulation of dominant theological concepts will manifest themselves in fissures, gaps, paradoxes, and incongruities on the surfaces of their expressions.

These markings index the incompleteness of the movement toward totalization and in this sense violate or transgress any law of closure in the symbolic order.

Fourth, a new agenda for theology is ironic. Extreme formulations that populate theological discourse convolute within the symbolic order so that they are instantiations of a transversal negativity implicating the other of the unthought and unrealized. That is, these formulations and figurations of ultimacy make demands upon textual and intertextual referencing that cannot be met. Lonergan's "the complete set of answers to the complete set of questions" and the "unrestricted desire to know," Anselm's "that than which nothing greater can be conceived," Tracy's use of the formulation "always already, not yet," and Tillich's identification with God as being-itself—all have a functional affinity with Scharlemann's understanding of instantiations of radical negativity. They are a mystery and aporia in the symbolic order. There is an irony in the theological agenda when it accepts as its task in analysis of "the being of God when God is not being god"[45]

Fifth, theology is text production. There is no special privilege to its discursive formations that comes from outside of the text production. The theological exigencies inscribed within its texts are effects of the metonymical placing of extreme formulations throughout the texts. The differential play of reference witnesses to that which is other than the text through the incompleteness that is the result of the placement of these formulations. Theological texts are not self-contained because of their internal undecidability.

Sixth, theology is a social text. Its subjectifications are material folds in specific social and historical locations. Its efficacy is in the pressure of its formulations upon ordinary usage and reference when they are metonymically forced into a discourse. The pressure of figurations of ultimacy on the pragmatics of discourse is a transvaluation of the ordinary. Theology is a social text that makes a claim upon the economy of forces and received texts that constitute its specificity through the particularity of its fold. Formulations and figurations of ultimacy when metonymically placed in a textual practice can fold the already existing folds of received texts.

In this sense a theological analysis introduces an incommensurability into discursive practices that is an internal trace of the other in the subjective fold of discourse. Theological practice even when framed by the ontotheological tradition can be aligned with the critique of logocentrism if its formulations are under- stood as metonymical strategies. There is an affinity with Der- rida's claim that "deconstruction is always deeply concerned with the 'other' of language. . . . The critique of logocentrism is above all else the search for the 'other' and the 'other of language'."[46] When deconstruction is part of the theological agenda the chal- lenge is always to deconstruct the greatest totality, and this means, as Gasché has suggested, repeating the totality while making it tremble.

Theology has a deconstructive agenda and deconstruction has a theological agenda. Deconstruction cannot repeat the totality of the ontotheological tradition in its totality without becoming implicated in theological exigencies in the formation of its dis- course. Theology in the articulation of its strategies can make a further move. Not only can theology in its deconstructive mo- ment make the totality tremble, make it insecure in its most as- sured evidences; but it can sustain the trembling as it folds its own interrogation into the textual and intertextual referencing of the symbolic order. The theological agenda is in its double folding a cultural agenda.

NOTES

Note: The sources of my epigraphs are, respectively: Jameson, *Marxism and Form: Twentieth Century Dialectical Theories of Literature* (Princeton: Princeton Univ. Press, 1971), p. xviii, and Friedrich Nietzsche, *The Will to Power*, trans. Walter Kaufmann and R. J. Hollingdale (New York: Vintage, 1968), p. 3.

1. John P. Muller and William J. Richardson, *Lacan and Language: A Reader's Guide to Ecrits* (New York: International Universities Press, 1982), p. 3.
2. Jane Gallop, *Reading Lacan* (Ithaca: Cornell Univ. Press, 1985), p. 46.
3. Ibid., p. 20.
4. Ibid., p. 117.
5. Jacques Lacan, *Ecrits: A Selection*, trans. Alan Sheridan (New York: Norton, 1977), p. 2.
6. Gallop, *Reading Lacan*, p. 59.
7. Ibid.
8. Ibid., p. 60.
9. Jacques Lacan, *The Four Fundamental Concepts of Psychoanalysis*, trans. Alan Sheridan (New York: Norton, 1978), p. 20.
10. Ibid., p. 21.
11. Ibid., p. 25.
12. Ibid., p. 153.
13. Ibid., p. 315.
14. Ibid., p. 26.

15. Michel Foucault, *Language, Counter-Memory, Practice,* trans. Donald F. Bouchard and Sherry Simon (Ithaca: Cornell Univ. Press, 1977), p. 42.
16. Michel Foucault, *The Order of Things: An Archaeology of the Human Sciences* (New York: Vintage, 1973), p. 318.
17. Ibid., p. 326.
18. Michel Foucault, *The Archaeology of Knowledge,* trans. A. M. Sheridan Smith (New York: Pantheon, 1972), p. 55.
19. Gilles Deleuze, *Foucault,* trans. Sean Hand (Minneapolis: Univ. of Minnesota Press, 1988), p. 104.
20. Ibid., pp. 104–5.
21. Frederic Jameson, *The Political Unconscious: Narrative as a Socially Symbolic Act* (Ithaca: Cornell Univ. Press, 1981), p. 152.
22. Karl Marx, "Theses on Feuerbach," in *The German Ideology: Part One with Selections from Parts Two and Three and Supplementary Texts,* ed. C. J. Arthur (New York: International Publishers, 1985), p. 121.
23. Mikhail Bakhtin, *The Dialogic Imagination: Four Essays,* ed. Michael Holquist (Austin: Univ. of Texas Press, 1981), p. 368.
24. Rodolphe Gasché, *The Tain of the Mirror: Derrida and the Philosophy of Reflection* (Cambridge: Harvard Univ. Press, 1986), p. 180.
25. See Paul Tillich, *The Future of Religions* (Chicago: Univ. of Chicago Press, 1966) and *Christianity and the Encounter with World Religions* (Chicago: Univ. of Chicago Press, 1963).
26. Paul Tillich, *Systematic Theology,* 3 vols. (Chicago: Univ. of Chicago Press, 1951, 1957, 1963) 2:10.
27. Friedrich Nietzsche, *The Gay Science,* trans. Walter Kaufmann (New York: Vintage, 1974), p. 182.
28. Tillich, *Systematic Theology,* 2:42–43.
29. Ibid., p. 61.
30. Ibid., p. 60.
31. Ibid., p. 36.
32. Ibid., p. 33.
33. Ibid., p. 92.
34. Ibid., 1:19.
35. Ibid., p. 166.
36. Ibid., p. 192.
37. Ibid., p. 18.
38. Ibid., p. 169.
39. Ibid.
40. Ibid., 2:11.
41. Ibid., 1:238.
42. Ibid., p. 239.
43. Paul Tillich, *The Dynamics of Faith* (New York: Harper Torchbooks, 1958), p. 46.
44. Tillich, *Systematic Theology,* 1:12.
45. See Robert Scharlemann, "The Being of God When God Is Not Being God," in *Deconstruction and Theology* (New York: Crossroad, 1982), pp. 79–108.
46. Richard Kearney, *Dialogues with Contemporary Continental Thinkers* (Manchester: Univ. of Manchester Press, 1984), p. 123.

3
_____

NOTHING ENDING

NOTHING

Nothing is final, he chants. No man shall see the end.
WALLACE STEVENS

True revolt is the one inspired by the impossibility of
ending.
EDMOND JABÈS

Perhaps you will be tempted to call this the disaster, the
catastrophe, the apocalypse. Now here, precisely, is announced—as promise or threat—an apocalypse without
apocalypse, an apocalypse without vision, without truth,
without revelation, of *dispatches* . . . , of addresses without messages and without destination, without sender or
decidable addressee, without last judgment, without any
other eschatology than the tone of the "Come" itself, its
very difference, an apocalypse beyond good and evil.
JACQUES DERRIDA

I experienced an atrocious pain, the most lively pain possible—it split my head open—but perhaps more lively
than alive; it is hard to express how it was at once cruel
and insignificant: a horrible violence, an atrocity, all the

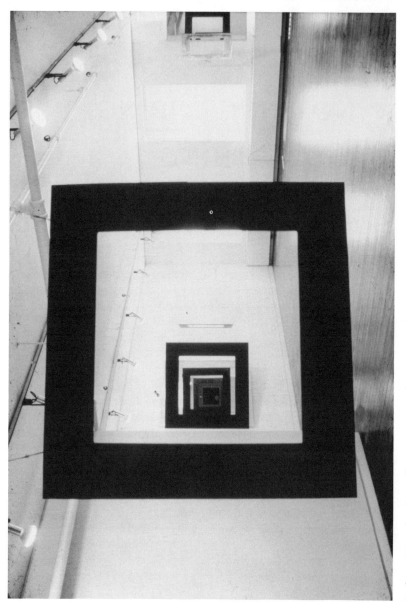

Robert Morris, *Installation*, 1976. (Courtesy the artist)

more intolerable because it seemed to come to me across
a fabulous layer of time, burning in its entirety inside
me, an immense and unique pain, as though I had not
been touched at this moment but centuries ago and for
centuries past, and the quality it had of being something
finished, something completely dead, could certainly
make it easier to bear but also harder, by turning it into a
perseverance that was absolutely cold, impersonal, that
would not be stopped either by life or by the end of life.

MAURICE BLANCHOT

Framing Questions

"FRAMING QUESTIONS." How to read? Which is subject: "framing," "questions"? Which is verb: "framing," "questions"? How to read? "Nothing ending nothing." Nothing ending . . . a beginning that is an ending, a nonending that keeps beginning? Ending nothing . . . an end of nothing, which, as such, does not end but goes on, and on, and on . . . ? "Nothing Ending Nothing." How to read . . . Titles . . . are frames. Frames that frame work. Frameworks—frame works. What is a framework? How do frames work? What is a frame? "Where does the frame take place. Does it take place? Where does it begin. Where does it end. What is its internal limit. Its external limit. And its surface between the two limits."[1]

. . .

"Framing questions." What if an essay were nothing . . . nothing but a title? What if a work were nothing . . . nothing but frame(s)? What if a work framed nothing but frames that frame nothing? Who would be framed? What would be framed?

Robert Morris's 1976 *Installation* consists of black frames that frame nothing. Three of the frames are suspended in an empty room with white walls. At a certain angle, one frame, which is large enough to walk through, frames two and a half other frames. The half frame is "within" a mirror that is hanging on a wall. From another angle, the mirror inverts and doubles the empty frames, thereby creating a labyrinthian framework. How to read . . . frame work? Morris offers no help. He is silent, always silent. The one who wanders through the vertiginous space of these frames has the sense of being read more than reading, being framed more than framing. But by whom or by what? There "is" nothing in the frames—nothing other than other more distant frames that frame other more distant frames.

.   .   .

"Framing questions." What if an essay had no title? Would it begin? Where would it begin? What if a work had no frame? Would it begin? Where would it begin? Would it end? Where would it end?

Yves Klein did not frame his works. Indeed, frames interrupt the goal of art, which, according to Klein, is the experience of unification for both artist and viewer. Klein is best known for his monochromatic paintings, most of which are a brilliant blue that eventually came to be known as "International Klein Blue." A carefully formulated metaphysical position informs Klein's painting. In a short text entitled "The Monochromatic Adventure," he writes: "As soon as there are two colors in a painting, combat begins; the permanent spectacle of this battle of two colors may give the onlooker a subtle psychological and emotional pleasure that is nevertheless morbid from a purely human, philosophical point of view."[2] To overcome such divisive combat, Klein removes all figuration and presents a single color on a frameless canvas. The experience of painting is, for Klein, essentially religious. A life-long follower of Rosicrucianism, Klein claims: "My goal was to restore lost Eden." The blue monochromes dissolve forms into an undifferentiated unity of color that reactualizes the primordial identity of subject and object. These paintings actually represent nothing. The nothingness of Klein's blue is, however, a curious nothing. Rather than the mere absence or negation of being, this blue embodies the plenitude of being's presence. So viewed, nothing is the no thing that is in all things. Klein's nonrepresentational monochromes are, in effect, painterly versions of classical negative theology. As the negative theologian "speaks" of God by saying what God is not, so Klein paints the ineffable by removing every trace of figure and contrast of color. "Through absolute art, i.e., the living illumination which I become by sealing myself in the worlds of works of art, by saturating myself with the eternal limitless sensitivity of space, I return to Eden, as I certainly feel; and this is why, in my art, I refuse more and more emphatically the illusion of personality, the transient psychology of the linear, the formal, the structural."[3] The end for which both theologian and painter strive is unitive ecstasy with the all.

Yves Klein, *Monochrome, International Klein Blue 43*, 1958. (Courtesy Sidney Janis Gallery, New York; photo by Allan Finkelman)

There is undoubtedly a messianic dimension to Klein's person and work. His aim is not only to achieve unity through painting; he also wants to draw others into the oneness with the totality for which he believes we all long. In an effort to accomplish this end, Klein frequently transforms his art into a public performance. One of his most extraordinary performative gestures was the "Exhibition of the Void," which took place on 28 April 1958 (Klein's thirtieth birthday) at the Galerie Iris Clert in Paris. Klein emptied the gallery of everything and painted it entirely white. The only thing in the gallery that was not white was a blue drink offered to guests as they entered. The exhibition created a considerable sensation. When more than two thousand people tried to squeeze into the small gallery, the police and fire department had to be called to avoid a riot. For Klein, the most important moment in the exhibition was the drinking of the blue cocktail, which he explicitly interpreted as an act of communion. "The blood of the body of sensibility," Klein declared, "is blue." What he did not tell the communicants was that the mixture of gin, cointreau, and methylene blue made them urinate blue for a week—the precise length of time for which the "Exhibition of the Void" originally was scheduled. Nowhere in modern art does the erasure of the frame reach such proportions. Thomas J. J. Altizer's remark on Barnett Newman might better be applied to the fullness of Klein's void: "When fully realized, as in the late paintings of Barnett Newman, abstract art seems to pass into nonart, for it dissolves the frame of the easel, passing into the world beyond it, and that world is a purely and totally anonymous world."[4]

When the margin of difference between interiority and exteriority collapses, unity becomes totally present. Blue—the blue of Eden—"impregnates" all, thereby giving birth to the concrete actualization of the all. As Klein's theological glosses on his work suggest, this total presence realizes the full incarnation of the sacred in the profane. Altizer's analysis again is helpful.

> At no point does it even hint of the presence of God as God, or of God as Word or Wisdom or "I." Nevertheless, no simple or literal anonymity is present here, and cannot be so present if only because we recognize our own ground and source in such a vision, and demonstrably recognize it in the very intensity and immediacy of our response. Only bad faith could refuse or evade such a vision as a vision in some sense of God, even if not of a uniquely singular and personal God. If we can but realize that not only a total vision but also a vision of totality is at least potentially present in modern art,

then we can realize that it will by necessity break through and transcend all singular and individual forms and images, including our given and historical images of God.[5]

The return to Eden is the apocalyptic union of Alpha and Omega. For Klein, the color of the apocalypse is *blue*. *Blue: "bhel*—shine; blaze, burn; shimmer like a flame; hence, move to and fro; hence, bright colors and objects."[6] The apocalyptic fire of blue consumes everything by returning all things to the no thing of the void in which emptiness is fullness.

.   .   .

"Framing questions." What if an essay were not whole but rent, not solid but hollow, not complete but incomplete? What if rending, hollowness, and incompletion were aftereffects of something like an unerasable frame that repeatedly interrupts as if from within in such a way that ending is impossible?

"Blue" harbors another trace—a trace that is less inflammatory, though no less disruptive; *kel*—"hollow; to cover; to hide. Greek. *kaluptein*; English, *conceal*. *Calypso* ("she who conceals"). Calypso, who interrupted Odysseus' return home, "lived in a deep cave with several rooms, which opened on wild gardens, a sacred wood with great trees and streams which flowed over the turf. She spent her time spinning and weaving with her serving girls."[7] *Kel* is also related to the Germanic *Hel*, which was the name of the hideous Norse goddess who rules over the dead.[8] Where are Calypso and Hel to be found in Eden? What rending, hollowness, and incompletion does International Klein Blue try to conceal?[9]

In 1958, while Yves Klein was mounting his "Exhibition of the Void," Lucio Fontana began a series of works entitled *"Tagli (Concetti spaziali—Attese)* [Cuts (spatial concepts—Expectation)]." These "cuts" were inflicted on monochromatic canvases that were usually white or gold and irregularly shaped. The tear in the canvas interrupts the plenitude of the formless void by creating an opening to a "beyond" that is (impossibly) both inside and outside the painted surface. It is not clear whether the incisions have been made from the front or the back of the painting. Fontana's

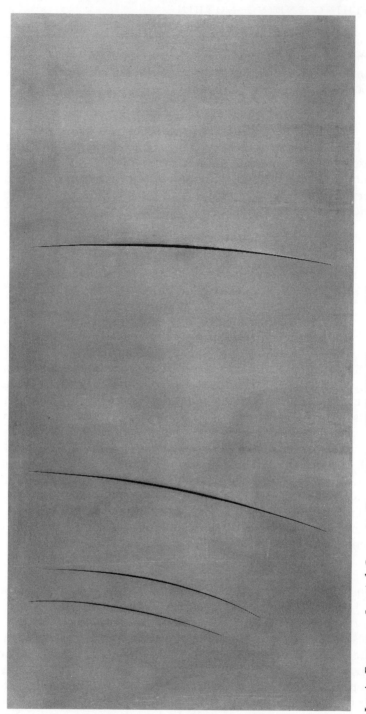

Lucio Fontana, *Spatial Concept, Expectations 59 T 133.* (Courtesy Solomon R. Guggenheim Museum, New York; photo by Robert E. Mates and Mary Donlon)

wounded canvases are no more representational than Klein's monochromes. The nothing of Fontana's *Tagli* is not, however, the same as the nothing of Klein's blue void. Rather than the no thing that *is* in all things, Fontana's nothing implies a lack of being that neither exists nor does not exist. The lack is (not) the absence of the frame but repeatedly remarks the frame "within" the work itself, thereby reinscribing precisely the margin of difference that Klein, like all modernists, struggles to erase or efface.

What does the lack depend on? What lack is it?
And what if it were the frame. What if the lack formed the frame of the theory. Not its accident but its frame. More or less still: what if the lack were not only the lack of a theory of the frame but the place of the lack of a theory of the frame.
Edge/lack [10]

"Framing questions." The question of the frame: How can this edge/lack be thought? How can it be written? The question of *das Gestell* points toward the task of thinking at the end of theology. [11]

. . .

Theology at the End . . . The End of the Twentieth Century. Is theology at the end of the twentieth century the end *of* theology? How to read? Is the end *of* theology a double genitive that spells both the dissolution and the completion of theology? Are all ends theological and thus every end the end *of* theology? What is an end? What is the end? If theology has reached *its* end, then what is the task of (theological) thinking?

The task of thinking at the end of theology is to think the end otherwise than as the end *of* theology by thinking ending a/theologically. Theology will have reached its end when it has thought (the) all and thus has nothing left to think. After thinking the all, the question that remains is how to think the nothing that theology has left unthought. If this unthought nothing is to be thought, it must not be thought ontotheologically. To think nothing non-ontotheologically would be to think an end that is not the end *of* theology. This end would not be an *apocalypse* but would be a *disaster*—a disaster that devastates (the) all by approaching without ever arriving. The difference between apocalypse and disaster is the difference between two readings of death. Within the "theological" register, the difference between apocalypse and disaster is

the difference between two readings of the death of God. As the
end of the twentieth century approaches (but will it ever arrive?),
the question of how to read the death of God becomes inescapable. Is the death of God the condition of the *possibility* of the
arrival of the Parousia or is it the condition of the *impossibility* of
the arrival of the Parousia? Does the death of God reveal that
nothing is ending or mark the impossibility of ending nothing?

Nothing Ending Nothing

What happens when the title that frames the work is reinscribed
(like a *Tagli*) "within" the text? Perhaps nothing. Nothing perhaps.

Scene of (Self-)Recognition

Dialogue and dialectics. Season the words of a dialogue (the division of voices); season then the intonations (of a personal and
affective character); shell abstract notions and reasonings from live
words and sayings; wrap the whole in a unique abstract consciousness—and you get dialectics.[12]

The end of theology is apocalyptic—inevitably apocalyptic. As
such, it is inextricably bound to death. The death of God is the
end of theology. This end is simultaneously the consummation
and the dissolution of the history of the Christian West. From a
dialectical point of view, the end is implicit in the beginning. Accordingly, history is an archeoteleological process in which the
Alpha and Omega gradually realize the relation in and through
which they are always already One. To appreciate the difficulties
and the opportunities for thinking at the end of theology, it is necessary to consider the end that guides the historical process from
its beginning.

In his remarkable book *History as Apocalypse*, Thomas J. J. Altizer argues that the history of the West begins with "the birth of
vision." The birth of vision, which is enacted and embodied in ancient Greek art, puts an end to the "primal anonymity" characteristic of prehistoric life that is graphically captured in the haunting
cave paintings of Lascaux. Altizer, following Jaspers and others,
identifies an "axial period" during which the crucial transition
from anonymity to individuality takes place:

In the eighth century B.C.E. a revolutionary transformation occurred in the ancient world, perhaps the most profound revolution

in history. It erupted simultaneously and apparently spontaneously in Greece, Israel, and India, and somewhat later in China and Iran. This was a comprehensive and radical breakthrough from the archaic world and consciousness to the birth of full and actual individual consciousness. While the modes and identities of this consciousness differed radically from each other in these disparate axial centers, each realized a primacy and finality of a truly new interior center of consciousness. . . . Only in Greece does one name embody this initial or original revolution, and that name is Homer. For even if *The Iliad* and *The Odyssey* evolved out of bardic traditions and schools, they are nonetheless fully individual and organic poems, and so much so that it is only with the advent of these poems that we can speak historically of the poet as creator. A decisive sign of the presence of the poet as creator is the birth of the poem as an integrated and unified whole or world, a world and a work which for the first time in history evolve out of its own center or ground, a ground deriving from a new center of consciousness which stands out from its own horizon and world.[13]

This new center of consciousness becomes concretely visible in Greek sculpture that dates from the sixth century. In the *Head of Apollo*, the faceless figures of the cave give way to the human eye whose vision "draws us into its new world of sight."[14] This world of vision, born in ancient Greece, comes to completion over two millennia later in Germany. What begins as the sight that establishes individual consciousness ends as the insight that secures transparent self-consciousness. Or so the (dialectical) story goes.

Western self-consciousness reaches closure in Hegel's speculative-specular philosophy. Hegel synthesizes Greek vision and Christian faith to produce a unity that realizes both the death of God and the birth of total self-consciousness. In the *Phenomenology of Spirit*, Hegel presents something like a bildungsroman in which he plots the interrelated development of both humanity as a whole and individual human beings as they progress toward the perfect self-consciousness that becomes possible with the advent of absolute knowledge. One of the crucial chapters in this story is the transition from consciousness to self-consciousness. In the concluding paragraphs of the opening section of the *Phenomenology*, Hegel first identifies the dialectical structure of self-consciousness and then proceeds to describe the moment of its emergence: "I *distinguish myself from myself,* and *in so doing I am immediately aware that what is distinguished is not different* [dies Unterschiedene nicht unterschieden ist]. I, the selfsame being, repel myself from myself; but what is posited as distinct from me, or as unlike me, is immediately, in being so distinguished, not a distinction for me."[15] When interpreted in this way, self-consciousness re-presents the logical structure that lies at the foundation of Hegel's entire System. As early as the *Differenz-schrift* Hegel describes this structure as the "union of union and nonunion." "The Absolute," he avers, "is the identity of identity and non-identity; being opposed and being one are both together in it."[16] Within the bounds of Hegel's speculative logic, the structure of subjectivity is the identity-within-difference in which the subject becomes *itself* in and through the relation to *its own* other. Nonunion, difference, and otherness are both necessary to and encompassable within the identity of the subject. Before the development of true self-consciousness, the subject mistakenly regards objectivity as different from and opposed to itself. Through a careful examination of various manifestations of objectivity, however, the subject gradually turns back on itself. When objects are no longer viewed as inert entities but are grasped as concrete appearances of general laws, consciousness discovers the identity-within-difference of objectivity and subjectivity. The lawful object is a unified plurality and a pluralized unity.

> Law [Hegel maintains] completes itself in an immanent necessity, and all the moments of appearance are taken up into the inner world. That the simplicity of law is infinity means . . . (a) that it is self-*identical*, but it is also in itself *different;* or it is the selfsame that repels itself from itself or sunders itself into two. . . . (b) The bifurcation, which represents the parts thought of as in the *law*, exhibits itself as subsistent. . . . (c) But through the notion of inner difference, these unlike and indifferent moments . . . are a *difference* that is no *difference*, or only a difference of what is *selfsame*, and its essence is unity. . . . The two differentiated moments both subsist; they are *in themselves* and are *opposites in themselves*, i.e., each in the opposite of itself; each has its other within it and they are only one unity.[17]

When conceptually comprehended, it becomes apparent that the object is formally homologous with the structure of subjectivity. In view of this isomorphism, the subject's cognition of the object is simultaneously its re-cognition of itself. Though at first convinced of the irrefutable otherness of the object, consciousness passes from sense-intuition and perception to understanding in which it realizes that its relation to the object is, in fact, self-relation.

> Raised above perception, consciousness exhibits itself closed in a unity with the supersensible world through the mean [*die Mitte*] of appearance, through which it gazes [*schaut*] into this background. The two extremes, the one of the pure inner world, the other that of the inner being gazing into this pure inner world, now have converged [*zusammengefallen*], and just as they, as extremes, have vanished, so too the mean as something other than the extremes, has also vanished. This curtain [*Dieser Vorhang*] hanging before [*vorhanden*] the inner world is therefore drawn away, and we have the inner [the subject] gazing into the inner [of the object]— the vision of the *undifferentiated* selfsameness [ununterschiedenen *Gleichnamigen*], which repels itself from itself, posits itself as an inner being containing differentiated moments, but for which equally these moments are immediately *not* different—*self-consciousness*.[18]

This scene of (self-)recognition is apocalyptic. Apocalypse (*apokalyptein*, uncover; *apo*, reversal + *kaluptein*, to cover) is always a matter of vision, sight, and insight. The seer penetrates illusory appearance and discovers naked truth hiding beneath the play of veils. When the subject strips away the "curtain" separating it from objectivity, it discovers nothing other than itself.[19] To lift this curtain is to erase the frame that differentiates inside and outside. In the absence of the frame, difference gives way to identity and otherness returns to same. As Altizer explains:

> Hence difference as difference becomes unsaid when it is fully spoken. But it is unsaid only in being actually unsaid. The silence of the unsaid is now actually spoken, and when it is fully spoken it passes into total speech. Total speech can only be the disembodiment, the actual negation, of difference. When speech is fully embodied in pure voice, it is disembodied from difference, or disembodied from all difference which is only difference. But that disembodiment from difference is also the full actualization of difference. Now difference is fully actual by having come to an end as difference, by having come to an end as a difference which is other and apart.[20]

Altizer offers this remark in the final chapter of *The Self-Embodiment of God*, which is entitled "Apocalypse." A drama in five acts, the self-embodiment of God ends with the death of the hero. The unsaying of difference is the death of God. In the fullness of *speech*, the divine "I AM" dies and is reborn in the human "I am."

> Then the voice of "I AM" is heard in the voice of "I am." That hearing is the resurrection of the voice of "I AM," but it is so only insofar as "I AM" is silent in "I am," or only insofar as the voice of resurrection is the voice of silence. When the voice of resurrection is the voice of silence, then the presence of speech is totally at hand, and totally at hand in the actuality of silence. Now silence is not only the embodiment of speech, it is the full actuality of speech, and the total actuality of speech, an actuality embodying all presence and embodying all presence in the fullness and finality of silence. When all presence is embodied in silence, then silence is all in all, and silence is all in all when it is both actually and totally heard.[21]

The death of God becomes actual as the absolute silence of transcendence. This silence, which echoes the *absence* of God, issues in the total *presence* of universal humanity, which now is deemed divine. If history "begins" with the emergence of individual consciousness from the anonymity of prehistory, it "ends" with the eclipse of individual consciousness in the anonymity of posthistorical presence.

> But ours is the time of the end of a unique and individual consciousness, and the end of that consciousness is the end of history as well, and the beginning of a posthistorical time when an integral and interior individuality will have disappeared. . . . For that interior is not truly or actually our own, and thus genuine solitude releases us from the power of our own interior, and in such moments we know and fully know that every interior which is our own has actually come to an end. But the real end or reversal of an individual interior makes possible the actual advent of a universal presence, a presence transcending all interior and individual identity, and presenting itself beyond our interior, and beyond every possible interior, as a total and immediate presence.[22]

This "total and immediate presence," according to Altizer, becomes fully actual in twentieth-century art. While Hegel insists that philosophy reveals the rational truth of art and religion, Altizer contends that religion and art realize the truth anticipated in

Hegel's philosophy. This truth is most fully present in Joyce's "apocalyptic" language. Altizer concludes *History as Apocalypse* by commenting on the language of *Finnegans Wake:*

> That speech is the real presence of resurrection, and its full enact-
> ment is the total presence of Apocalypse, a presence in which the
> dark and negative passion of God becomes immediately at hand.
> And it is immediately at hand insofar as it is actually spoken. Then
> the total silence and emptiness of an original abyss becomes [*sic*]
> an immediately present chaos which is cosmos when it is res-
> urrected in language and word. This cosmos is the resurrected
> Christ, but a resurrected Christ who is inseparable and indistin-
> guishable from the crucified Christ, for now the Christ of glory *is*
> the Christ of passion. So it is that the body of this Christ can only
> be a dark and broken body, but it is a body which is present in all
> the immediacy of an unformed and primordial matter, as a totally
> fallen body now realizes itself in the pure immediacy of the word.
> In that immediacy death is life, and "Lff" is all in all.[23]

When death is life, and Lff is all in all, nothing remains to be thought. Here theology reaches *its* end. To think "beyond" this end, it is necessary to think an end that is not the end *of* theology. This end cannot lie "outside" theology but must dwell "within" as an irreducible exteriority that cannot be assimilated. To think the nothing that remains to be thought at the end of theology is to think unendingly.

Living It

> It was only a hole
> in the wall
> so narrow that you never
> could have gotten into it
> to flee.
> Beware of dwellings. They are not always hospitable.[24]

A thinker erects a huge building, a system, a system embracing the whole of existence, world history, etc. and if his personal life is con-
sidered, to our amazement the appalling and ludicrous discovery is made that he himself does not personally live in this huge, domed palace but in a shed, or in a doghouse, or at best in the janitor's quarters. Were he to be reminded of this by one single word, he

would be insulted. For he does not fear to be in error if he can only complete the system—with the help of being in error.[25]

Can one live the unity or harmony that Hegel has thought? Or is the System, as Kierkegaard was quick to realize, a fantastic palace that is uninhabitable? Toward the end of his life, Hegel came to doubt that the harmony he envisaged had been historically realized. He ends his famous Berlin lectures on the philosophy of religion on a "discordant note": "But this reconciliation is itself only a partial one, lacking outward universality. Philosophy forms in this connection a sanctuary apart, and those who serve in it constitute an isolated order of priests, who need not mix with the world, and whose work is to preserve the possession of truth. How the empirical present day is to find its way out of its discord, and how things are to turn out for it, are questions that must be left up to it and are not the immediate practical business and affair of philosophy."[26] But perhaps what was merely possible in the nineteenth century has become historically (or, more precisely, posthistorically) actual as we draw near the end of the twentieth century. So Altizer would seem to have us believe. As I have suggested, however, the death of God can be read otherwise. If one rethinks the end of theology, the death of God might imply the impossibility instead of the realization of total presence. The words of the *Wake* might, then, mourn an inescapable absence or impossible presence rather than celebrate a *missa jubilaea*.

In the end, Joyce's vision fails. If, as Altizer insists, the history of the West begins with "the birth of vision" and ends with Joyce's *Finnegans Wake,* this closure seems to entail blindness and not insight. As blindness descends, Joyce no longer could speak for himself but had to speak through an other. Unable to write, Joyce was forced to dictate much of *Finnegans Wake* to Samuel Beckett. Beckett, the other in whose writing Joyce speaks, is never himself, for he is always haunted by an other he cannot name or can name only improperly: "But I don't say anything, I don't know anything, these voices are not mine, nor these thoughts, but the voices and thoughts of the devils who beset me."[27] Beckett's insight presupposes a certain blindness that interrupts (the) vision of the eye/I of Western reason. To hear the other murmuring endlessly in Beckett's texts is to suffer the approach of the nothing that theology leaves unthought.

This unsettling nothing is inscribed in *The Unnamable* as (the) unnamable. *The Unnamable* is the final work in a trilogy that can be read as a parodic undoing of Hegel's three-part System. Taken together, *Molloy, Malone Dies,* and *The Unnamable* reverse the triadic movement of Hegelian speculation. While Hegel charts a dialectical progression that expands as comprehension grows, Beckett narrates a nondialectical contraction that becomes less and less comprehensible. Instead of presenting the movement from isolated individuality to universal humanity, Beckett recounts the decline from manhood to Mahood in which we first encounter a character who retains a semblance of identity and can still explore city streets and forests, then a dying man whose forced immobility restricts him to a single room, and finally a limbless body propped up and stuck in a jar. The consciousness that inhabits this grotesque body presents what at first appears to be a monologue but is eventually exposed as a complex dialogue in which Beckett effectively overturns Hegel.[28] While the dialogue that Hegel creates among different forms of consciousness turns out to be a monologue in which Absolute Spirit speaks to itself, Beckett's monologue becomes a dialogue in which the subject of self-consciousness discovers the discourse of an other that cannot be named. This other is an outside that is inside, forever displacing the total self-presence requisite for transparent self-consciousness.

From the time of his youthful master's thesis on Descartes, Beckett is preoccupied with the question of the subject. *The Unnamable* opens with a confession of doubt concerning the subject: "Where now? Who now? When now? Unquestioning. I, say I. Unbelieving. Questions, hypotheses, call them that."[29] To say "I" unbelieving is to call into question the certainty of the Cartesian ego as well as the absolute knowledge of the Hegelian subject. Within Hegel's System, certainty becomes truth through a process of reflection in which objectivity is grasped as the self-objectification of the creative subject. To become itself, the subject enacts a process of self-exile and return in the course of which it recognizes *itself* in every other.

> That the true is actual only as system, or that substance is essentially subject, is expressed in the representation of the Absolute as *Spirit*—the most sublime notion and the one that belongs to the modern age and its religion. The spiritual alone is the *actual*; it is essence, or that which has *being in itself*; it is that which *relates itself to itself* and is *determinate*, it is *other-being* and *being-for-*

self, and in this determinateness, or in this self-externality, abides within itself; in other words, it is *in and for itself*.[30]

By contrast, Beckett's narrator in *The Unnamable* cannot recognize himself in any of his self-objectifications: "Why did I have myself represented in the midst of men, the light of day? It seems to me it was none of my doing. We won't go into that now. I can see them still, my delegates. The things they have told me! About men, the light of day. I refused to believe them. But some of it has stuck. But when, through what channels, did I communicate with these gentlemen? Did they intrude on me here? No, no one has ever intruded on me here. Elsewhere then. But I have never been elsewhere."[31] For Beckett, the subject forever eludes the economy of representation. "Delegates," which fail to represent properly, leave the subject disenfranchised. Never present, but always "elsewhere," the self cannot re-present itself to others or even to itself. In the absence of self-reflection, all the Murphys, Molloys, and M-alone-s are merely "a waste of time."

> There, now there is no one here but me, no one wheels about me, no one comes towards me, no one has ever met anyone before my eyes, these creatures have never been, only I and this black void have ever been. And the sounds? No, all is silent. And the lights, on which I had set such store, must they too go out? Yes, out with them, there is no light here. No grey either, black is what I should have said. Nothing then but me, of which I know nothing, except that I have never uttered, and this black, of which I know nothing either, except that it is black and empty. That is what, since I have to speak, I shall speak of, until I need speak no more.[32]

"Nothing then but me, of which I know nothing." To know nothing of oneself is to have no identity—absolutely no identity. In the absence of identity, the narrator charges: "It's the fault of the pronouns, there is no name for me, no pronoun for me, all the trouble comes from that, that, it's a kind of pronoun too, it isn't that either, I'm not that either, let us leave all that, forget about all that, it's not difficult, our concern is with someone, our concern is with something, now we're getting it, someone or something that is not there, or that is not anywhere."[33]

The self itself, it seems, is unnamable. More precisely, the subject is haunted by "someone or something that is not there, or . . .

anywhere." This someone or something encrypted "within" the self interrupts the self's relation to itself and displaces all identity. The subject harbors an irreducible difference that leaves it forever faulted. "I'm something quite different, [the narrator sighs,] a quite different thing, a wordless thing in an empty place, a hard shut dry cold black place, where nothing stirs, nothing speaks."[34] "Nothing stirs, nothing speaks" through the discourse of an other that is an exteriority lodged "within" the subject. This other doubles the subject, rendering it incurably duplicitous. The self is never itself but is always at the same time an other it cannot know. Though never present as such, the inescapable double is not simply absent. It is, in Blanchot's terms, a "nonabsent absence." This duplicitous absence can be heard—if at all—in what Beckett describes alternatively as an inarticulate "murmur" or simply "noise."[35] "I sum up, now that I'm there, it's I will do the summing up, it's I will say what is to be said and then say what it was, that will be jolly, I sum up, I and this noise, I see nothing else for the moment."[36] The articulate speech of the cognitive ego struggles vainly to silence this disruptive noise. In its lapses and hesitations, through its slips and gaps, language carries the faint echo of what it can neither express nor contain. Inasmuch as this murmur is always stirring, it is, in a certain sense, "older" than the speaking subject. "Agreed, agreed, I who am on my way, words bellying out my sails, am also that unthinkable ancestor of whom nothing can be said. But perhaps I shall speak of him some day, and of the impenetrable age when I was he, some day when they fall silent, convinced at last I shall never get born, having failed to be conceived. Yes, perhaps I shall speak of him, for an instant, like the echo that mocks, before being restored to him, the one they could not part me from."[37] Never simply itself, the subject is (impossibly) always "older" than itself. This "impenetrable age" is what Blanchot describes as the "terrifyingly ancient" and Levinas labels the "unrepresentable before." Since it is always already "present" as "absent," the "impenetrable age" that marks the subject as an "unthinkable ancestor" cannot be represented in or by self-consciousness. The past that radically ages the subject by forever doubling it is an absolute past that never was or will be present. In a text that bears a striking resemblance to *The Unnamable*, Blanchot explores this uncanny past.

"Sometimes she is far away, very far away," she said, making an impressive gesture with her hand.

"In the past?" I asked timidly.

"Oh, much farther away!"

I pondered, trying to discover what could really be farther away than the past. Meanwhile, she seemed all of a sudden afraid that she had thrown me slightly beyond the limits.[38]

What is "farther away than any past" is so *near* to the present that it can never be represented. The remote proximity of this past throws one "slightly beyond the limits" of language. Commenting on Blanchot, Foucault indirectly illuminates the duplicity of *The Unnamable:*

The companion is not a privileged interlocutor, some other speaking subject; he is the nameless limit language reaches. That limit, however, is in no way positive; it is instead the deep into which language is forever disappearing only to return identical to itself, the echo of a different discourse that says the same thing, of the same discourse saying something else. "Celui qui ne m'accompagnait pas" ("he who did not accompany me") has no name (and wishes to remain cloaked in that essential anonymity); he is a faceless gazeless *he* who can only see through the language of another whom he submits to the order of his own night; he edges as close as can be to the *I* that speaks in the first person, and whose words and phrases he repeats in an infinite void. Yet there is no bond between them; an immeasurable distance separates them. That is why he who says *I* must continually approach him in order finally to meet the companion who does not accompany him and who forms no bond with him that is positive enough to be manifested by being untied. There is no pact to tie them to each other; yet they are powerfully linked by a constant questioning . . . and by the uninterrupted discourse manifesting the impossibility of responding. It is as if this withdrawal, this hollowness that is perhaps nothing more than the inexorable erosion of the person who speaks, cleared a neutral space of language. The narrative plunges into the space between the narrator and the inseparable companion who does not accompany him; it runs the full length of the straight line separating the speaking *I* from the *he* he is in his spoken being; it unfolds a placeless place that is outside all speech and writing, that brings them forth and dispossesses them, that imposes its law on them, that manifests through its infinite unraveling their momentary gleaming and sparkling disappearance.[39]

At the edge of language, the subject loses (its) identity. With everything turned inside out and outside in, the self is neither one nor many but is the "hollow," "neutral space"—a "placeless place that is outside all speech and writing."[40] In one of the most re-markable passages in his entire corpus, Beckett suggests that this placeless place is the impossible locus of the ever elusive subject.

> Perhaps that's what I feel, an outside and an inside and me in the middle, perhaps that's what I am, the thing that divides the world in two, on the one side the outside, on the other the inside, that can be as thin as foil, I'm neither one side nor the other, I'm in the middle, I'm the partition, I've two surfaces and no thickness, per-haps that's what I feel, myself vibrating, I'm the tympanum, on the one hand the mind, on the other the world, I don't belong to either, it's not to me they're talking, it's not of me they're talking, no, that's not it, I feel nothing of all that, try something else.[41]

. . . the thing that divides the world in two . . . as thin as foil . . . neither one side nor the other . . . the middle . . . the partition . . . no thickness . . . I'm the tympanum . . . vibrating . . . re-verb-erating.

But what is a tympanum? A tympanum, which derives from *steu* (knock, beat, thrust, push) by way of the Greek *tympanon* (a drum), is something like a membrane. This membrane can serve as a musical instrument, that is, a tambourine, timbrel, or drum, or as the organ of hearing, that is, the eardrum. Architecturally, a tympanum is the recessed, ornamental space or panel enclosed by the cornices of a triangular pediment that often serves as the en-trance to a cathedral. In French, the other language in which Beckett writes, *tympaniser* means to decry, criticize, or ridicule publicly. Derrida prefaces *Margins of Philosophy* with an essay entitled "Tympan." This preface begins (after three epigraphs from Hegel) not with a sentence but with a fragment. "To tym-panize—philosophy."[42] To tympanize philosophy is to criticize it—to hold it up to public ridicule by exposing the faults that in-evitably lead to its failure. The failure of philosophy is marked by the tympan, which is the margin of discourse that philosophy pre-supposes but cannot comprehend.

> If there are margins, is there still *a* philosophy, *the* philosophy? No answer, then. Perhaps, in the long run, not even a question.

> The copulative correspondence, the opposition question/answer is already lodged in a structure, enveloped in the hollow of an ear, which we will go into to take a look. To find out how it is made, how it functions. And if the tympanum is a limit, perhaps the issue would be less to displace a *given* determined limit than to work toward the concept of limit and the limit of the concept.[43]

What goes out from the mouth returns through the ear. For knowledge to be complete or absolute and hence transparent self-consciousness possible, this circle of expenditure and return cannot be broken. At the site of passage between inside and outside, however, there now appears to be a tympanum, which functions like a frame that simultaneously brings together what it holds apart and holds apart what it brings together. The frame is the displaced and displacing "between" that opens the space or creates the clearing for the differences that constitute identity. Rather than a site proper, the frame is the parasite (*le parasite*, interference) that both facilitates and interrupts the circuit of exchange through which messages are sent and received. The reverberations of the tympanum mark the return of disquieting questions that must be reframed. "(Re) framing questions." The question of the frame: How can this edge/lack/margin/tympan be thought? How can *it* be written? Perhaps, Blanchot suggests, in the work of art.

> And indeed what *The Unnamable* depicts is this malaise of one who has dropped out of reality and drifts forever in the gap between existence and nothingness, incapable of dying and incapable of being born, haunted by the phantoms he creates, in which he does not believe and which refuse to communicate with him. But neither is this the whole answer. The whole answer should rather be found in the process by which the work of art, seeking its realization, constantly reverts to the point where it is confronted with failure. The point where language ceases to speak but is, where nothing begins, nothing is said, but where language is always reborn and always starts afresh.[44]

If language "is always reborn and always starts again," the work of art is endless. The end, in other words, never arrives but is forever delayed. The narrator in *The Unnamable* "ends" by declaring the impossibility of ending: "Where I am, I don't know, I'll never know, in the silence you don't know, you must go on, I can't go on,

I'll go on."[45] Language ceases to speak in and through its failure—
a failure that is never complete. The failure of language is the
"lack" that frames discourse. Rather than searching for a plenitude that would fulfill the economy of representation, the writer
struggles to inscribe the lack of language by allowing words to fail.

> The problem . . . is that the inadequqcy of language . . . runs the
> risk of never being sufficiently inadequate. The lack of language:
> what this means (to begin with) is two things—a lack with respect
> to what has to be signified, but at the same time a lack that is at the
> center and the life of meaning, the reality of speech (and the rela-
> tionship between these two lacks is itself incommensurable). To
> speak—as we know today—is to bring this kind of lack into play,
> maintain it and deepen it in order to make it *be* more and more,
> and in the end what it puts in our mouths and under our hands is
> no longer the pure absence of signs but the prolixity of an indefi-
> nitely and indifferently signifying absence: a designation that re-
> mains impossible to annul, even if it carries nullity within it.[46]

"The prolixity of an indefinitely and indifferently signifying absence" . . . "I can't go on, I'll go on." When language ceases to
speak by failing unendingly, "nothing begins, nothing is said."
Saying nothing traces a disaster that is not apocalyptic.

Disaster of Death

> Of gaps was the spirit of these redeemers made up; but into every
> gap they put their delusion, their stopgap, which they called God.[47]

If God is, in effect, a stopgap measure, then the death of God
would seem to leave gaps gaping. Instead of leading to the total
presence constitutive of the actualized Kingdom, the death of
God might subvert the very possibility of the arrival of the Parousia by forever deferring the realization of presence. From this
point of view, to declare the death of God is to affirm the impossibility of the end.

For Altizer, the end is not only possible but has already arrived.
The end, we have seen, becomes actual in the full presence em-
bodied in modern art. This presence can only be enjoyed in what
Altizer describes as "absolute solitude." The final chapter of *Total*

Presence is entitled "The Solitude of the End." The penultimate paragraph of the book begins with the following words: "Genuine solitude is a voyage into the interior, but it is a voyage which culminates in a loss of our interior, a loss reversing every manifest or established center of our interior so as to make possible the advent of a wholly new but totally immediate world."[48] The end, like the beginning, is anonymous. The solitude of the end is the death rather than the birth of individual consciousness. The transcendent God and the isolated subject are mirror images of each other. The death of God is the disappearance of the individual self and vice versa. Within the circular economy of salvation, however, death is rebirth. As God dies and is reborn in man, so individual interior consciousness dies and is resurrected in "a universal presence, a presence transcending all interior and individual identity." When Alpha and Omega are One, distance, otherness, and difference disappear. The *Self-Embodiment of God* ends with "Apocalypse": "The speech of total speech can only be the speech of total presence. But how can total presence be actually present? How can it be present in actuality? . . . Now the actual voice of total speech must be without a center or a source which is distant and apart. Distance disappears in total presence, and so likewise does all actual otherness which is not the otherness of that presence itself."[49] The solitude of the end is not *my* solitude but is the solitude of the One with which my death unites me. When the One is all in all, solitude is absolute. Then and only then can (the) One declare, "It is finished."[50] In the presence of this One, nothing remains.

"Nothing remains." How to read . . . how to write . . . after the death of God and the end of theology? If theology has reached *its* end, then what is the task of thinking? The task of thinking at the end of theology is to think the end otherwise than as the end *of* theology. An end that is not an end *of* theology would be an end that is never present—an end that *does not*, indeed *cannot* arrive. Such an endless end is a disaster for (ontotheological) thought:

"*When all is said, what remains to be said is the disaster. Ruin of words, failure by writing, faintness faintly murmuring: what remains without remains* (the fragmentary)."[51] As Beckett suggests and Blanchot contends, "the ruin of words, failure by writing" is the work of art. The work of art is neither to present nor to represent but to enact the impossibility of presence and stage the failure of re-presentation. The placeless place of this performance is "the space of literature."

The space of literature marks a t-*raum*-a that leaves gaps gaping. Blanchot, like Altizer, is preoccupied with solitude. What Blanchot discovers in solitude, however, is not redemptive presence but a doubling of the subject that makes unity impossible. He begins an important fragment entitled "The Essential Solitude and Solitude in the World" by observing:

> When I am alone, it is not I who am there, and it is not from you that I stay away, or from others, or from the world. I am not the subject to whom this impression of solitude would come—this awareness of my limits; it is not that I tire of being myself. When I am alone, I am not there. This is not a sign of some psychological state, indicating loss of consciousness, the disappearance of my right to feel what I feel from a center that I myself would be. What approaches me is not my being a little less myself, but rather something that is there "behind me," and that this "me" conceals in order to come into its own.[52]

What is this "something that is there 'behind me,'" which, when not concealed by me, prevents the self from coming into its own? It is nothing other than the "terrifyingly ancient" that we have already encountered as the "impenetrable age" of the unnamable. By receding in an absolute past, that is, a past that was never present, this ancient something paradoxically approaches as an absolute future, that is, a future that never arrives. The guise of this ancient future is *death*. As the future that never arrives, death is the end of the end.

To insist that death is the always outstanding future is to maintain that death is, in a certain sense, impossible. And yet nothing seems more contrary to both common sense and philosophical reflection than to claim that death is impossible. Death seems to be the one possibility that all living beings share. In the wake of Heidegger's existential meditations, the awareness of the possibility of *one's own* death has become definitive of human authenticity.[53] But is death ever our *own*? Or is the effort to own death a struggle for mastery in which the subject attempts to become itself by overcoming the most terrifying other?

The possibility of death takes two forms that correspond to the contrasting rhythms of *thanatos*. *Thanatos*, as Freud points out, involves either division and separation or unification and reunion. Accordingly, the possibility of death appears either to define or erase individuality. The most extreme expression of death as a

possibility for an individual is suicide. In suicide, a person attempts to overcome the future by taking possession of death. "He
who kills himself, "Blanchot argues, "is the great affirmer of the
present. I want to kill myself in an 'absolute' instant, the only one
that will not pass and will not be surpassed. Death, if it arrived at
the time we choose, would be an apotheosis of the *instant;* the
instant in it would be that very flash of brilliance of which the
mystics speak."

> By committing suicide, I want to kill myself at a determined mo-
> ment. I link death to now; yes, now, now. But nothing better indi-
> cates the illusion, the madness of this "I want," for death is never
> present. There is in suicide a remarkable intention to abolish the
> future as the mystery of death: one wants in a sense to kill oneself
> so that the future might hold no secrets, but might become clear
> and readable, no longer the obscure reserve of indecipherable death.
> Suicide in this respect does not welcome death; rather, it wishes to
> eliminate death as future, to relieve death as that portion of the
> yet-to-come that is, so to speak, its essence, and to make it super-
> ficial, without substance and danger.[54]

To abolish the future in the now—the present instant—is to affirm the reality of the presence for which mystics long. At this
moment, in this moment, the divisive impulse of *thanatos* reverses itself in a movement of "return to the transfigured whole."[55]

The desire to die can also be understood as the longing for fulfillment that expresses "a certain need for plenitude." Apart from
death, there is no totality. "The affirmation that in man all is possibility requires that death itself be possible: death itself, without
which man would not be able to form the notion of an 'all' or to
exist in view of a totality, must be what makes all—what makes
totality possible."[56] The death of the self *is* the life of the whole.
This whole is the all-encompassing totality that incorporates difference and assimilates otherness. In the presence of this apocalyptic totality, one discovers that "death is life, and 'Lff' is all
in all."[57]

But what if death *is not* possible but forever remains impossible? What if the future of death *is* absolute and thus never becomes present? Though death approaches, it never arrives; though
it is near, it is not present. Where death is, I am not, and where I
am, death is not. "One never dies now, one always dies later, in
the future—in a future that is never actual, that cannot come except when everything will be over and done. And when every-

thing is over, there will be no more present: the future will again be past. This leap by which the past catches up with the future, overstepping the present, is the sense of human death, death permeated with humanity."[58]

The terrifyingly ancient that was never present approaches as the absolute future that never arrives. This metalepsis of past and future "oversteps" the present. In the nonabsent absence of death, time is not the moment of mystical presence but is "time without a present." "Death's rightful quality is impropriety, inaccuracy— the fact that it comes either too soon or too late, prematurely and as if after the fact, never coming until after its arrival. It is the abyss of present time, the reign of a time without a present, without the exactly positioned point that is the unstable balance of the instant whereby everything finds its level up to a single plane."[59] Forever implicated in "a time without a present," "death can never become an event." Death is (but, of course, it is not) the nonevent that is "the dissolution of every event."[60] In the abyss of the present, the impossibility of the event of death becomes the "event" of the impossible. Rather than leading to salvation or eternal life, the impossibility of death implies its unending proximity. So understood, death is the disaster that never arrives. In Blanchot's terms, "The disaster is the impossibility of death. . . . There is no end."[61]

The disaster is not the apocalypse. It is not a matter of vision, sight, or insight. The nonsite of the disaster is not a scene of (self-) recognition. No veils are stripped, no curtains raised, no skirts lifted. The disaster "reveals" *nothing*. This nothing is not the nothing of ontotheology. The nothing of the disaster, in other words, is *neither* the no thing that is the fullness of being *nor* the absence of things that is the emptiness of nonbeing. The nothing that both philosophy and theology leave unthought is "between being and nonbeing."[62] It neither is nor is not; it is not present without being absent. Nothing approaches by withdrawing and withdraws by approaching. Through its approach, nothing ends ending by insuring that nothing ends. If, as the poet chants, "nothing is final," nothing is final.

The disaster, then, is the nonevent in which nothing happens. The eventuality of nothing ruins all presence by interminably delaying the arrival of every present.

> The disaster ruins everything, all the while leaving everything intact. It does not touch anyone in particular; "I" am not threatened by it, but spared, left aside. It is in this way that I am threatened; it

is in this way that the disaster threatens in me that which is exterior to me—an other than I who passively become other. There is no reaching the disaster. Out of reach is he whom it threatens, whether from afar or close up, it is impossible to say: the infiniteness of the threat has in some way broken every limit. We are on the edge of disaster without being able to situate it in the future: it is rather always already past, and yet we are on the edge or under the threat, all formulations that imply the future—that which is yet to come—if the disaster were not that which does not come, that which has put a stop to every arrival.[63]

If the end cannot arrive, apocalpyse is impossible. By ending ending, the disaster is something like "an apocalypse without apocalypse." "Perhaps you will be tempted to call this the disaster, the catastrophe, the apocalypse. Now here, precisely, is announced—as promise or threat—an apocalypse without apocalypse, an apocalypse without vision, without truth, without revelation, of *dispatches* . . . , of addresses without destination, without sender or decidable addressee, without last judgment, without any other eschatology than the tone of the 'Come' itself, its very difference, an apocalypse beyond good and evil."[64]

The nonapocalyptic end of the disaster is an end that is no longer the end *of* theology but an end that lies "beyond" the closed economy of the ontotheological tradition. The absence of the end has a retroactive effect on the beginning, even as the inaccessibility of the beginning harbors an aftereffect for the end. If God is the Alpha and the Omega, then the death of God marks the end of the beginning as well as the end. The impossible future of death is but the mask of the disastrous past that hollows out every thing and every one as if from within. The past that was never present eternally returns as the future that never arrives to disrupt the present that never is. The absence of presence is inscribed in the nonrepresentational work of art.[65] With the work of art, we return to the beginning—*without* having come full circle.

A Return to the Question

But where has art led us? To a time before the world, before the beginning. It has cast us out of our power to begin and to end; it has turned us toward the outside without intimacy, without place, without rest. It has led us into the infinite migration of error. . . . It ruins the origin by returning it to the errant immensity of an eternity gone astray.[66]

When eternity goes astray, nothing remains . . . but nothing . . . to think (or to think not) . . . endlessly . . . by writing . . . the disaster . . . errantly . . . in a writing that writes nothing.

The death of God is the betrayal of God. Death betrays . . . always betrays . . . for it always comes too soon or too late. In the absence of God, death betrays nothing.

> For the listener, who listens in the snow,
> And, nothing himself, beholds
> Nothing that is not there and the nothing that is.[67]

"Nothing that is not there and the nothing that is." The nothing that "remains without remaining" after the death of God or as the death of God creates a bind that is a double bind.

Religion is a binding (*ligare*) back (*re*) that is supposed to bind together. The return to the origin that constitutes the end holds out the promise of unifying human life by reconciling opposites and overcoming strife. If, however, the end never arrives . . . If God is dead . . . If the origin is always missing, then religion binds back to nothing. When *re-ligare* fails by returning (the) all to nothing, it must be repeated. Through repetition, binding back is transformed into a re-binding that creates a double bind. This double bind is the trace of the nothing that is betrayed by the death of God. To be bound to and by nothing is not to be free but is to be entangled in a double bind from which there is no escape. In the aftermath of the death of God, religion no longer heals wounds by binding together the opposites that tear apart. To the contrary, religion exposes wounds that can never be cured. The "re-" of religion marks a repetition (compulsion) that neither solves nor heals but re-marks the devastating space that is the dead time of the nonapocalyptic disaster. The wake/*Wake* that (interminably) mourns the death of God must find a way to betray the betrayal of God. "And man must understand the sacred sense of this divine infidelity, not by opposing it, but by performing it himself."[68] The betrayal of God betrays the sacred. Such duplicitous betrayal cannot be represented theologically but must be performed a/theologically. To write the impossibility of theology by writing an a/theology in which God is always missing, it is necessary to rethink the death of God by thinking the way one dies.

> To die without end: thus (through this movement of immobility) would thought fall outside all teleology and perhaps outside its site. To think endlessly, the way one dies—this is the thinking that

patience in its innocent perseverance seems to impose. And this
endlessness implies not gratuity but responsibility. Whence the repeated, motionless step of the unknown without language, there at
our door, on the threshold.

To think the way one dies: without purpose, without end, without power, without unity, and precisely, without "how," without
"the way." Whence the effacement of this formulation as soon as it
is thought—as soon as it is thought, that is, both on the side of
thinking and of dying, in disequilibrium, in an excess of meaning
and in excess of meaning. No sooner is it thought than it has de-
parted; it is gone, outside.[69]

To think the way one dies: without purpose—errantly—without
end—endlessly.

> Wisdom asks nothing more.[70]

> Nothing more
>   More nothing
> Nothing ending
>   Ending nothing
> Nothing Ending Nothing

Framing Questions

"Nothing ending nothing." Nothing ending . . . a beginning that
is an ending, a nonending that keeps beginning? Ending nothing . . . an end of nothing, which, as such, does not end but goes
on, and on, and on . . . ? "Nothing Ending Nothing." How to
read . . . Titles . . . are frames. Frames that frame work. Frameworks . . . frame works. What is a framework? How do frames
work? What is a frame? "Where does the frame take place. Does it
take place. Where does it begin. Where does it end. What is its
internal limit. Its external limit. And its surface between the two
limits." What if an essay were not whole but rent, not solid but
hollow, not complete but incomplete? What if rending, hollowness, and incompletion are aftereffects of something like an unerasable frame that repeatedly interrupts as if from within in such
a way that ending is impossible?

> *Tagli (Concetti spaziali—Attesse)*
> Cuts (spatial Concepts—Expectation)

Enrique Espinosa, *The Silence of Jesus.* (Courtesy the artist)

The question of the frame: How can the edge/lack/margin/
tympan be "written"?

> My design represents only the edge of body of The Crucified. I used
> two plates separated by negative space, at the center you can see an
> empty space—that emptiness is the shape of Jesus. The negative
> space is a window you can see through, you have to discover Him.
> Every time and culture has created a way to represent Jesus. I did it
> with the empty space that frames our circumstances.[71]

"The empty space that frames our circumstance": "The Silence
of Jesus." Silence is not the mere absence of words but is the endless failure of language. This failure is the sacrifice of the Word
that betrays the betrayal of God.

The silence of Jesus

apocalypse without apocalypse

. . . *dispatches* . . . addresses without message . . . without destination . . . without sender . . . without decidable addressee . . .

à Dieu

adieu

.

. . .

.

NOTES

1. Jacques Derrida, *The Truth in Painting*, trans. G. Bennington and I. McLeod
   (Chicago: Univ. of Chicago Press, 1987), p. 63.
2. Yves Klein, "The Monochromatic Adventure," *Yves Klein, 1928–1962: A
   Retrospective* (Houston: Institute for the Arts, Rice University), p. 220.
3. Ibid., p. 224.
4. Thomas J. J. Altizer, *Total Presence: The Language of Jesus and the Language
   of Today* (New York: Seabury, 1980), pp. 32–33.
5. Ibid., p. 35.
6. Unless otherwise indicated, etymologies are from Joseph T. Shipley, *The Origins of English Words* (Baltimore: Johns Hopkins Univ. Press, 1984).

7. Pierre Grimal, *Dictionary of Classical Mythology*, trans. A. R. Maxwell-Hyslop (London: Basil Blackwell, 1986), p. 87.
8. See H. R. Ellis Davidson, *Scandinavian Mythology* (New York: Paul Hamlyn, n.d.).
9. There is a strange relationship between the color blue and some of the most important modern and postmodern works of art. Consider, inter alia, Picasso's blue period, *Der blaue Reiter*, and Georges Bataille's *The Blue of Noon*. To my knowledge, no one has explored the implications of the role blue plays in these vastly different works.
10. Derrida, *The Truth in Painting*, pp. 42–43.
11. See Martin Heidegger, "The End of Philosophy and the Task of Thinking," *On Time and Being*, trans. J. Stambaugh (New York: Harper and Row, 1972), pp. 55–73. It is not insignificant that this essay first appeared in a volume dedicated to Kierkegaard.
12. Mikhail Bakhtin, quoted in Tzvetan Todorov, *Mikhail Bakhtin: The Dialogical Principle*, trans. W. Godzich (Minneapolis: Univ. of Minnesota Press, 1984), p. 104.
13. Thomas J. J. Altizer, *History as Apocalypse* (Albany: State Univ. of New York, 1985), p. 19.
14. Ibid., p. 22.
15. G. W. F. Hegel, *Phenomenology of Spirit*, trans. J. N. Findlay (New York: Oxford Univ. Press, 1977), p. 102. For some reason, Findlay omits the italics in his translation.
16. G. W. F. Hegel, *The Difference between Fichte's and Schelling's System of Philosophy*, trans. H. S. Harris and W. Cerf (Albany: New York Univ. Press, 1977), pp. 88, 91. For a more complete analysis of Hegel's dialectical logic, see Mark C. Taylor, *Journeys to Selfhood: Hegel and Kierkegaard* (Berkeley and Los Angeles: Univ. of California Press, 1980), esp. chap. 5.
17. Hegel, *Phenomenology of Spirit*, pp. 99–100.
18. Ibid., p. 103.
19. Derrida underscores some of the implications of the word *apocalypse* when he writes: "*Apokalupto* no doubt was a good word, a witticism [*bon mot*] for *gala. Apokalupto*, I disclose, I uncover, I unveil, I reveal the thing that can be a part of the body, the head or the eyes, a secret part, the genitals or whatever might be hidden, a secret, the thing to be dissembled, a thing that does not show itself or say itself, that perhaps signifies itself but cannot or must not first be handed over to its self-evidence. *Apokekalummenoi logoi* are indecent remarks. So it is a matter of the secret and the *pudenda*. The Greek language shows itself hospitable here to the Hebrew *gala*. As André Chouraqui recalls in his short 'Liminaire pour l'Apocalypse' of John . . . , the word *gala* recurs more than a hundred times in the Hebrew Bible. And it seems in effect to say *apokalupsis*, disclosure, discovery, uncovering, unveiling, the veil lifted from the truth revealed about the thing: first of all, if we can say this, men's or women's genitals, but also their eyes or ears" ("Of an Apocalyptic Tone Recently Adopted in Philosophy," *Semeia* 23 [1987]: 64).
20. Thomas J. J. Altizer, *The Self-Embodiment of God* (New York: Harper and Row, 1977), p. 82.
21. Ibid., p. 93.
22. Altizer, *Total Presence*, pp. 102, 107.
23. Altizer, *History as Apocalypse*, p. 254.
24. Edmond Jabès, quoted by Jacques Derrida, "Ellipsis," *Writing and Difference*, trans. A. Bass (Chicago: Univ. of Chicago Press, 1978), p. 298.
25. Søren Kierkegaard, *The Sickness unto Death: A Christian Psychological Exposition for Upbuilding and Awakening*, trans. H. V. Hong and E. H. Hong (Princeton: Princeton Univ. Press, 1980), pp. 43–44.

26. G. W. F. Hegel, *Lectures on the Philosophy of Religion*, vol. 3, ed. P. C. Hodg-son (Berkeley and Los Angeles: Univ. of California Press, 1985), p. 162n.
27. Samuel Beckett, *The Unnamable* (New York: Grove Press, 1978), pp. 83–84.
28. I do not mean to suggest that Hegel is a direct target of Beckett's narratives. To the contrary, his critique (if that is what it is) is always implicit and indirect.
29. Beckett, *The Unnamable*, p. 3.
30. Hegel, *Phenomenology of Spirit*, p. 14.
31. Beckett, *The Unnamable*, p. 12.
32. Ibid., p. 21.
33. Ibid., p. 164.
34. Ibid., p. 139.
35. In this context, it is interesting to note that "noise" derives from the Latin "*nausea*, seasickness (with extended senses in popular use, e.g., 'unpleasant situation,' 'noisy confusion')" (*American Heritage Dictionary*). The irrepres-sible noise that bombards Beckett's narrator is not only confusing but even-tually becomes nauseating. In an effort to create a sense of nauseous confusion in the reader, Beckett's prose gradually disintegrates. After the first few pages of the text, there are no more paragraphs. Toward the end of the work, sen-tences unravel as the prose approaches vertiginous babel.
36. Beckett, *The Unnamable*, p. 142. On the murmur: "Ah but the little murmur of unconsenting man, to murmur what it is their humanity stifles, the little gasp of the condemned to life, rotting in his dungeon garrotted and racked, to grasp what it is to have to celebrate banishment, beware" (p. 52).
37. Ibid., p. 91.
38. Maurice Blanchot, *When the Time Comes*, trans. L. Davis (Barrytown, N.Y.: Station Hill Press, 1985), p. 48. In view of the relationship between the abso-lute past and the feminine that Blanchot suggests here and elsewhere, it is im-portant to recall that Beckett's trilogy begins in the the space of the mother: "I am in my mother's room. It's I who live there now. I don't know how I got there. Perhaps in an ambulance, certainly a vehicle of some kind. I was helped. I'd never have got there alone (*Molloy*, trans. P. Bowles [New York: Grove Press, 1965], p. 7). From one point of view, it is possible to interpret all of Beckett's narrators as engaged in the struggle to return to this inaccessible space.
38. Michel Foucault, "Maurice Blanchot: The Thought from Outside," *Foucault/Blanchot*, trans. B. Massumi (New York: Zone Books, 1987), pp. 51–52.
40. This "hollowness" marks the return of the "rending, hollowness, and incom-pletion," which, we have observed, International Klein Blue tries to conceal.
41. Beckett, *The Unnamable*, p. 34.
42. Jacques Derrida, "Tympan," *Margins of Philosophy*, trans. A. Bass (Chicago: Univ. of Chicago Press, 1980), p. x. "Tympan" is not exactly included within the book entitled *Margins*. As a preface to the text, "Tympan" functions as something like the margin of *Margins*. Derrida underscores the liminality of "Tympan" by using Roman rather than Arabic numerals for this essay.
43. Ibid., pp. xvi–xvii.
44. Maurice Blanchot, "Where Now? Who Now?" *The Sirens' Song*, ed. G. Josipo-vici (London: Harvester Press, 1982), p. 197.
45. Beckett, *The Unnamable*, p. 179.
46. Maurice Blanchot, *The Gaze of Orpheus*, trans. L. Davis (Barrytown, N.Y.: Station Hill Press, 1981), p. 129.
47. Friedrich Nietzsche, *Thus Spoke Zarathustra*, *The Portable Nietzsche*, ed. Walter Kaufmann (New York: Penguin Books, 1968), p. 204.
48. Altizer, *Total Presence*, p. 106.
49. Altizer, *The Self-Embodiment of God*, p. 81.
50. These are the words with which Altizer concludes *The Self-Embodiment of*

God. This end is not, however, the end. So far two books and numerous articles by Altizer have followed "the end."

51. Maurice Blanchot, *The Writing of the Disaster,* trans. A. Smock (Lincoln: Univ. of Nebraska Press, 1986), p. 33.

52. Maurice Blanchot, *The Space of Literature,* trans. A. Smock (Lincoln: Univ. of Nebraska Press, 1982), p. 251.

53. Blanchot explicitly reject's Heidegger's analysis of death when he writes: "It is death as the extreme of power, as my most proper possibility, but also the death that never comes to me, to which I can never say yes, with which there is no authentic relation possible. Indeed, I elude it when I think I master it through a resolute acceptance, for then I turn away from what makes it essentially inauthentic and the essentially inessential. From this point of view, death admits of no 'being *for*-death'; it does not have the solidity with which to sustain such a relation" (*The Space of Literature,* p. 155).

54. Ibid., pp. 103, 104.

55. Ibid., p. 111.

56. Ibid., p. 130n., 240.

57. James Joyce, quoted in Altizer, *History as Apocalypse,* p. 254.

58. Blanchot, *The Space of Literature,* p. 165.

59. Ibid., p. 117.

60. Ibid., pp. 113, 241.

61. Blanchot, *The Sirens' Song,* p. 26.

62. Blanchot, *The Writing of the Disaster,* p. 14.

63. Ibid., p. 1.

64. Jacques Derrida, "Of an Apocalyptic Tone Recently Adopted in Philosophy," p. 94. See also Jacques Derrida, "No Apocalypse, Not Now (full speed ahead, seven missiles, seven missives)," *Diacritics,* 14, no. 2 (1984): 20–31.

65. For more extensive accounts of Blanchot's view of art, see Mark C. Taylor, *Altarity* (Chicago: Univ. of Chicago Press, 1987), and *Tears* (Albany: State Univ. of New York Press, 1989).

66. Blanchot, *The Space of Literature,* p. 244.

66. Wallace Stevens, "The Snow Man," *Collected Poems* (New York: Knopf, 1981), p. 10.

68. Blanchot, *The Space of Literature,* p. 272.

69. Blanchot, *The Writing of the Disaster,* p. 39.

70. Wallace Stevens, *Opus Posthumous,* ed. Samuel French Morse (New York: Random House, 1982), p. 158.

71. Personal correspondence from the artist. This sculpture is on display in the Vatican. Its site is suggestive. "The Silence of Jesus" is located in what the artist describes as "a provisional space" outside the Asian Exhibition and near the entrance to the underground Historic Museum.

THOMAS J. J. ALTIZER

4

THE BEGINNING AND ENDING OF REVELATION

REVELATION BEGINS with the self-naming of I AM, a self-naming which is not only the beginning of divine or ultimate speech, but therein and thereby is the release and the embodiment of total actuality, an actuality which is itself the origin of a full and total releasement. That releasement is what we have known as history, an actuality enacting once and for all or unique events, events which happen once and no more, and therefore events which can never be repeated or renewed. Yet having been once, though only once, such events have an actuality that otherwise would be absent, an actuality inseparable from the very ultimacy of their perishing. Only in the wake of the revelation of the divine name have events stood forth and been real in the actuality of their perishing, a perishing fully as ultimate as is the voice of I AM, and a perishing which is inescapable insofar as it occurs and is internally manifest. The very ultimacy of the embodiment of the divine name is a once-and-for-all releasement, a releasement bringing an end to the omnipresent silence of the unsaid, and in that ending perishing itself becomes fully actual, an actuality which is a final loss of an original silence.

The self-naming of I AM is the fullness and the finality of speech itself, a finality finally ending an original and total silence, and therefore and thereby finally ending an original quiescence. That ending is the beginning of a full and final actuality, an actuality which is perishing itself, and a perishing which we know as history. For the advent of history is the advent of death, and not simply the beginning of a real consciousness of death, but rather the beginning of a consciousness that is inseparable from death, and that not in its periphery, but rather in its center and core. Such death is not only an inescapable actuality, it is far rather actuality itself, an actuality which is the releasement of once and for all and unique events, which themselves are actual and real as the embodiment of death, or as the embodiment of a life that is the other side of death. Once the divine name has fully and finally been pronounced, to be open to the speaking of that name is to be open to actuality itself, an actuality which is the perishing of all life which is not life and death at once. A hearing of I AM is a hearing of that actuality, a hearing itself embodying actuality, and therefore a hearing embodying the presence of perishing and death. History is that presence, a presence which is the consequence of the self-embodiment of I AM, a self-embodiment apart from which neither history nor death would be actual and real.

If the beginning of history is the beginning of fall, that fall is the beginning of the revelation of I AM, a beginning which is not only itself a once and for all and unique event, but a beginning releasing once and for all and unique events, events which are fully actual in their very perishing, and events whose very perishing is their full and final actuality. That perishing is not only a consequence of the revelation of I AM, it is an embodiment of that revelation, an embodiment of the fullness and the finality of the voice of I AM, a finality which now is present as actuality itself. The releasement of that actuality is the revelation of I AM, a revelation which is the embodiment of I AM, and therefore the total presence of I AM. For the revelation of I AM is the full presence of the voice of I AM, a presence which is the absence of the unspeakability of I AM, and that absence can only be a fall from plenitude itself. Speech itself is inseparable from the loss of silence, and the speech or revelation of I AM is inseparable from the loss of the unspeakability of pure transcendence, an unspeakability which is inseparable from an original and total transcendence. Hence that transcendence perishes when revelation occurs, or when a unique and actual revelation occurs, an occurrence inseparable from a unique and once-and-for-all event. The self-naming of I AM in a unique and actual revelation is inevitably a loss of an original and total transcendence, and hence a fall from that transcendence, a fall which is the self-emptying of pure transcendence. That self-emptying can only be fall, a fall from the plenitude of an original transcendence, but a fall which is itself the irreversible beginning of a full and final actualization.

Nothing is more distant from an irreversible beginning than an eternal cycle of return, and if the myth of eternal return is the paradigmatic center of archaic and primordial worlds, the myth of a once and for all and irreversible beginning is the paradigmatic center of an irreversible historical world, a world that is the inevitable consequence of the self-revelation of I AM. Within no other horizon of consciousness do events stand forth and become manifest as unique and nonrepeatable events, events which happen only once, but whose sheer occurrence has a finality which is imperishable. That finality is inseparable from an irreversible beginning, a beginning which can never be repeated or renewed, and therefore a beginning whose finality is irrevocable. And it is irrevocable as beginning itself, a beginning which can never pass into an ending, as beginning does in a cycle of eternal return. Just as nothing finally distinguishes beginning and ending in a myth of eternal return, so a once-and-for-all beginning is beginning alone, an absolutely unique beginning, and a unique beginning which is the origin and ground of irreversible and unique events. Apart from that ground, events can neither be final nor unique, and then events as such can never be events which are fully and only themselves. Only in the wake and in the horizon of the self-revelation of I AM do events appear and become manifest as events which are individually and uniquely themselves, and that wake and that horizon are consequences of an irreversible beginning, a once-and-for-all beginning which can occur once and only once, and once that occurrence has entered the center of consciousness, consciousness itself becomes fully and finally closed to all events which eternally repeat and renew themselves in a cycle of eternal return.

But with the closure of the cycle of eternal return, ending becomes manifest and real as an irrevocable death, a death that is itself and no other, and therefore a death that never can pass into life. Yet the advent of irrevocable death is herewith and thereby the advent of a final actuality, an actuality inseparable from unique and unrepeatable events, and an actuality bestowing upon life itself the finality of an inescapable and irrevocable death. Consequently, the finalities of life and death are inseparable, as the advent of irrevocable death bestows upon life itself a new finality, a finality never hitherto present, and a finality inescapable for a consciousness knowing the ultimacy of death. Once such life has become manifest and real, nothing is more forbidden than a longing for death, a death that now and for the first time appears and is real through the full darkness of chaos itself. Now chaos appears as a chaos which is only itself, an original abyss which can never be sanctified or renewed in a cycle of eternal return, and a final abyss which is eternally closed to the presence of light. But the manifestation of that chaos is a decisive sign, of the presence of a new life, a life liberated from the encompassing power of a primordial abyss that can be the giver of life, as the appearance of the final and total darkness of chaos shatters the enticing and beckoning power of every primordial source and ground. Now death is otherness itself, a death that is wholly other than life, and with the realization of that death the life-giving power of the call of eternal return is ended.

Not until the self-revelation of I AM is the call of eternal return truly challenged, now that challenge occurs through a radical iconoclasm, an iconoclasm shattering every image and sign of a primordial abyss and night. That iconoclasm is a consequence not of the epiphany of I AM, but rather of the speech of I AM, for that speaking which is the self-naming of I AM is speaking and speaking alone, a pure speech foreclosing the very possibility of vision. Thereby speech itself gains an identity that it never had before, as primal speech is not only dissociated from myth and rite, but precisely thereby is liberated from every actual possibility of repetition. The words of I AM can never actually be repeated or resaid by another voice, and it is this very advent of an absolutely unique speech which brings with it the possibility of hearing a word which is itself and no other, a possibility apart from which the words of I AM could not be heard. But those words were heard, and their hearing ultimately issued in the ending of eternal return, an ending which is the beginning of the impact of irreversible events upon consciousness, an impact which ever more gradually and more fully called forth the release of individual and unique identities. Only now does a once-and-for-all and irreversible beginning become manifest and real, and only now does world itself become the arena and the horizon of ultimate praxis, a praxis releasing the ultimacy of primordial and sacred acts and events into the actuality of life and world itself.

Although it was only in the course of centuries that the impact of the self-revelation of I AM would be fully realized, its beginning was irreversibly established, and irreversibly established as the beginning of the ending of eternal return. If what we know as history is a realization of that revelation, then so likewise is the advent of the full actuality of the world itself, an actuality ever more fully manifest as the closure or erasure of everything beyond or apart from the world and time. Thereby concrete and irreversible events gain a gravity and finality that is truly new, as all the life and energy that once was invested in sacred and mythical realms is ever more fully given to the brute actuality of world itself. Such a reversal of energy did not occur immediately or at once, nor was it confined to a singular history or histories, or evolve in a unilinear manner and mode, or even in the West as opposed to the East. But evolve it did, even if in multiple movements and identities, and in forms often wholly disparate from each other, until finally realizing a global embodiment in the twentieth century. Such a momentous transformation could not be unrelated to that revelation which is surely its initial source, and even if that relation is a pure negation it is not a simple negation, but rather a negation incorporating and realizing that self-negation which is the origin and the ground of the self-naming of I AM.

The very speech of I AM is a self-negation of an absolute transcendence which itself is unspeakable, and unspeakable by virtue of total transcendence itself, a transcendence infinitely distant from and wholly other than any voice which could actually and immediately speak. Only in Israel did the scandal arise of a wholly transcendent and eternal voice fully speaking in an individual and unique voice, and the very occurrence of that voice is undeniable, or undeniable in terms of the revolutionary transformations which it effected. Revolution itself begins with that voice, or, at least, there is no evidence of an earlier beginning of a reversal of high and low, a reversal inverting all established forms of order and authority. Nothing is clearer or more decisive than the manifest and obvious truth that the revelation of I AM is a revolutionary reversal of all archaic and primordial worlds, and is so not only in its own words and voice, but equally so in the hearing which that voice and speech calls forth, a hearing negating everything in the hearer which is not attentive and wholly attentive to this speech occurring here and now, and occurring in actual and immediate words. Therein and thereby the hearer is hurled out of every center which is not present and actual here and now, which is not fully and immediately present in the horizon of speech. That hearing ends a center which is everywhere, and ends it by hearing a center which is wholly here and now, and wholly here and now in an actual and immediate voice whose own self-naming realizes itself as a total presence.

That total presence could only be the self-negation of eternal and transcendent presence, for it is a presence not only occurring here and now, but wholly occurring here and now, and occurring in the immediacy of a unique and actual voice. If this occurrence initially realizes a unique actuality, it also and even thereby releases actuality itself, an actuality which for the first time is immediately and totally present, and totally present in a once-and-for-all and irreversible event. That event is inevitably a reversal of eternal presence, and is so precisely because it is a once-and-for-all and unique event, an event that is the very opposite of eternal and transcendent presence. Accordingly, an enactment of a once-and-for-all event is a negation of transcendent presence, and a self-negation of that presence, or a self-negation of its own eternal ground. Apart from a negation of that ground, there could be no actualization of an irreversible event, a once-and-for-all event in which eternity is fully present, and fully and totally present in this actual and unique event. Thus it is that the self-revelation of I AM is the self-emptying of an eternal and transcendent presence, an emptying of the absolute ubiquity of eternal presence, as that presence is fully actual here and now, and totally present in the final actuality of an irreversible and once-and-for-all event. And that event is not only an irreversible event, but also an irrevocable event, and irrevocable in the very finality of its actuality, a finality embodying the ultimacy of eternity itself.

That ultimacy is present in the voice of I AM, and totally present in that voice, a presence that is present here and now, and totally present here and now. But the totality of that presence is inseparable from the emptying of an eternal and transcendent presence, an emptying apart from which there could be no actual total presence, no total presence here and now. That presence begins in the self-naming of I AM, and it irreversibly begins, a beginning occurring once and no more, and occurring with an ultimacy that never can be undone, an ultimacy embodying a final and total act. That is the act of revelation, the self-revelation of I AM, as I AM reveals itself in a full and total act, an act that never can be undone, and therefore an absolutely irreversible act, an act that never can be cancelled or dissolved. For to question the possibility of the dissolution of this act is to question the ultimacy of revelation itself, and not only to question it but to deny it, for here revelation is ultimate or it is not revelation at all. So likewise to question the ultimacy of such revelation is to question the finality of once-and-for-all and irreversible events, events which happen once and no more, and events which never can be undone. Here, beginning occurs, and it irreversibly occurs, occurring as the beginning of the self-emptying of transcendent presence, a self-emptying which is the full and actual self-negation of eternal and transcendent presence.

That self-negation is manifest in the advent of irreversible events, events which are fully actual, and fully actual in the fullness and finality of their occurrence here and now, an actuality embodying the ultimacy of total presence. I AM is the name of the origin of that presence, and the name of its beginning as well, a beginning which is the beginning of actuality itself, or the beginning of a total presence which is an actual presence. It is absence which is negated in such presence, and not only the absence of transcendent presence, but the absence of all nonactual presence as well. For with the realization of the self-emptying and self-negation of transcendent presence the ground of pure transcendence and pure otherness is annulled, and that annulment realizes the groundlessness of every presence which is not an actual presence, of every presence which is not present here and now. So it is that the self-negation of transcendent presence is the pure negation of absence itself, as the self-emptying of an original plenitude empties nonpresence itself, or empties its deep and ultimate ground, an emptying which is the advent of a pure and total actuality. The advent of that actuality is a consequence of the loss of an original presence, the loss of an original presence which is an eternal presence, an eternal presence which is everywhere, and is everywhere because it is nowhere as an actual and immediate presence. That is the everywhere which perishes when I AM speaks, and perishes in the actuality of that speech, an actuality which is fully and finally present here and now.

But the speech of I AM is the speech of an original presence, or, rather, the speech of an original presence here realizing an actual presence, for it is the self-emptying of an original presence which realizes the speech of I AM. An original and an eternal presence undergoes self-negation in the actual self-naming of I AM, a self-negation necessary and essential to the very utterance of ultimate speech, as ultimate speech actually speaks here and now. That actual speech is the intrinsic otherness of an original and eternal presence, but it is the intrinsic otherness of that eternal presence, and therefore the self-naming of I AM is the reversal or inversion of an original and eternal presence, a reversal in which the self-emptying of eternal presence is the realization of that presence here and now. If the realization of that presence realizes actuality itself, then the realization of actuality is the actual realization of eternal presence, and an eternal and transcendent presence becomes embodied as an actual presence. And that actual presence is imbued with the ultimacy and finality of an eternal presence, so that the full actuality of actual presence is the actualization of eternal presence, an actualization in which an eternal and transcendent presence realizes its own actual presence. Now even if that realization is the actualization of transcendent presence, it is not simply and only the presence of transcendent presence, but rather a presence in which transcendent and eternal presence is absent from and other than itself as eternal and transcendent presence, an absence here occurring as an ultimate and irrevocable act.

That act is beginning, an actual and irreversible beginning, and a beginning embodying the ultimacy and the finality of eternal presence. But it is an actual beginning and therefore it is not an ending, or it is an ending only insofar as it inaugurates the ending of an eternal and transcendent presence, and that ending is, indeed, the advent of a final and irrevocable beginning. If beginning and ending are one and continuous in a cycle of eternal return, and one and indistinguishable in an eternal and transcendent presence, they are intrinsically other in actual presence, and intrinsically other if only because an actual beginning irrevocably begins. That is a beginning which shatters the quiescence of eternal presence, and shatters it once and forevermore, as quiescence perishes in the very advent of an irreversible and irrevocable act. That act inaugurates a final ending, but it only inaugurates it, it only begins it, a beginning which as an actual beginning is intrinsically other than an actual ending. Now even if an actual beginning is inseparable from an actual ending, it is nevertheless distinguishable from that ending, and wholly distinguishable from an actual ending which is its essential and intrinsic opposite. For ending is the opposite of an actual beginning, and even if an actual beginning must culminate in ending, it does so only when it fully and finally ceases to be itself.

Now if beginning is ending in a primordial and eternal presence, and is realized as such in a cycle of eternal return, an actual beginning can realize an actual ending only by undergoing an ultimate transformation of itself, a transformation in which beginning must actually perish as beginning, and perish in a real and actual death. That death is a fully actual and once-and-for-all event, and a purely actual event, an event which is the culmination of an irreversible beginning. That beginning realizes itself in actual perishing, a perishing which is a full realization of an original irreversibility, and full realization because now that irreversibility is totally confirmed and fulfilled in the brute actuality of death itself. Yet this brute actuality is also and even thereby a final and ultimate actuality, as death itself now occurs as a once-and-for-all event, a once-and-for-all event in which alone death is and only is itself. True, the actuality of death is inaugurated with the advent of irreversible beginning, but it is only inaugurated thereby, an inauguration which precisely because it is a beginning is not yet and cannot yet be a full consummation. That consummation occurs in a death which is fully and finally death, and fully and finally death in the ultimacy of its occurrence, a death which is nothing less than the death of eternity itself. That is the death which inevitably had always been the destiny of an irreversible and irrevocable beginning, a beginning which necessarily must end, and end in the consummation of its own beginning.

Death is that consummation, and an ultimate and final death, a death which is just as irreversible and irrevocable as is an actual beginning, and a death which is thereby and precisely thereby a once-and-for-all event. For that death is the very opposite of the death which is celebrated in archaic cycles of eternal return, such primordial death returns or is resurrected as life itself, a life which is the other side of an eternal cycle of life and death, and a life that is no more actual than is a moment of eternal return. This is a life and death which can eternally be repeated and renewed in a cycle of eternal return, a cycle which itself annuls the very possibility of concrete and irreversible events, and it is in that very annulment that a cycle of eternal return realizes and fulfills itself. But this is the cycle and this is the return which is finally annulled in the once-and-for-all event of ultimate death. This is that death and that death alone from which there can be no return, for even if the perishing inaugurated by an irreversible beginning is a perishing realizing itself in the actuality of life and the world, it is not yet a death which can never be hidden or forgotten, not yet a death which is always present at the center of consciousness. Now death is that center, and a fully actual center, a center which now is the center of I AM.

If the self-naming of I AM is an actual reversal of an eternal and transcendent presence, and a reversal occurring in a once-and-for-all and irreversible event, then the consummation of that self-naming is the consummation of that reversal, a reversal fully and finally inverting eternal presence. That inversion is the actual death of eternal presence, and the ultimate death of eternal presence, a death which is a once-and-for-all event, and a death which is an irreversible and irrevocable event. But that event is the consummation of the revelation of I AM, and of the self-revelation of I AM, a self-revelation which is the final realization and actualization of I AM. Now death has an actuality that it never had before, a full and final actuality, but therewith and thereby actualization fulfills and transcends itself, a transcendence inaugurating the actuality of final ending. That final ending is, of course, the inevitable destiny of an irreversible and irrevocable beginning. And it is so not as the annulment but rather as the fulfillment of beginning, and the fulfillment of an irreversible and irrevocable beginning, for it is the beginning of actuality itself. That beginning can only be fulfilled in ending, but in an actual and ultimate ending, an ending which is the utter perishing of I AM. I AM is finally and actually itself in that ending, for the ending of revelation is the ending of I AM, and that fulfillment of revelation is the fulfillment of I AM.

Thus the fulfillment of revelation occurs in the death of I AM, the full and final death of I AM, a death which is at once a once-and-for-all and irreversible event and an absolute reversal of the cycle of eternal return, a reversal bringing eternal return to a final and ultimate end. That ending is an actual ending, and it ends the very possibility of return, as a final closure now occurs of every opening to eternal and transcendent presence, a closure which ever gradually but nevertheless finally affects an absolute transformation of history. The ground of this absolute transformation is precisely the closure of all ways of return, the closure of every actual opening to archaic and primordial worlds, and therewith the closure of every possible actual way to eternal and transcendent presence. Now even if such closure induces or effects compulsive quests for a realization of actual ways of eternal return, such ways can never now realize an actualization of return, as the ultimate death of I AM finally forecloses the very possibility of an eternal return. Then the actual realization of a reverse or backward movement of consciousness or history becomes impossible, and for the first time a truly and finally forward movement is established and becomes real, a forward movement which is irresistible and irrevocable by virtue of the finality of its embodiment.

That embodiment ever more gradually realizes itself in history, and even if it is met with innumerable countermovements and cycles of reaction, and thereby generates in Western Christianity the most dichotomous religious movement in history, the very actualization of such profound resistance and opposition finally has the effect of only carrying forward the absolute transformation of history. One decisive sign of the ultimate power of this movement and process of absolute transformation is the very advent of Christianity; never before or since has a historical movement occurred which initially realizes itself with such internal and interior violence, a violence generating a depth of internal conflict without parallel in history, and issuing in the most immediate and radical transformation of a movement which has ever occurred in history. That transformation itself is a clear sign of the absolute historical transformation now released in the world, and it was inevitably followed by the violent and dichotomous conflicts of Western history, a history which is now established as a total process of transformation. Moreover, it is a forward movement of transformation, a movement with a unique and actual beginning, and a movement inevitably and necessarily destined to a unique and actual ending. And that ending must inevitably be the very opposite of its beginning, the opposite of the beginning of an absolutely forward movement of consciousness and history.

The awareness and consciousness of a forward and total movement of history first occurs in apocalypticism, and here it is accompanied, and necessarily accompanied, by a ground in an absolute and total ending, an ending of world itself or of that which now can be named as old creation, an old creation which is the intrinsic opposite of new creation, and which must wholly and finally perish if new creation or the Kingdom of God is fully and finally actualized. Now if Jesus was the first prophet to proclaim the actual advent of the Kingdom of God, and if this advent was at the very center of his parabolic teaching and eschatological proclamation, then that advent could only be heard as an absolute assault upon the world, as an absolute negation of old creation, a negation apart from which there could be no actual advent of the Kingdom of God. This is the very negation which is actually realized with the advent of an absolutely forward movement of history, a movement impossible of realization apart from a negation of the past, and a movement whose very actualization inevitably brings with it a dissolution of the past. That is a dissolution which inevitably effects a realization that it is impossible to recover the past, and even if this realization is not fully real until the birth of the modern world, it is nevertheless true that the very beginnings of the Christian consciousness in Paul and the Fourth Gospel know a past which is intrinsically "other," and a past and a historical past which is the intrinsic opposite of grace and light.

Apocalypticism is at the very center of Western history, a center which is established with the birth of Christianity, and a center which is ever more fully realized throughout the multiple expressions of the Western consciousness, for this is the center which is the primal ground of historical revolution, a revolution which becomes global and universal in the twentieth century. And historical revolution, a revolution not born until the Middle Ages, revolves about an absolutely forward and an absolutely total movement of history, a movement that can realize itself only by negating the totality of the past, and a movement that even now knows itself as being the advent of the new creation. So it is that historical revolution is a historical consequence of primitive Christianity, just as the revolutionary movements of Western and now universal history are historical consequences of the birth of Christianity, for it is the very essence of genuine historical revolution that it intends and wills an absolute transformation of history. That transformation is an embodiment of the forward movement of history, a forward movement which is a total movement, and a total movement even now present as the dawning of the new creation. That creation is infinitely distant from and wholly other than the old creation, and its very advent is the decisive sign that the old creation has come to an end, and come to its end in its very center, a center which now is no more and never will be again.

That is the center which is finally ended with the actual death of I AM, an I AM whom the discourses of the Fourth Gospel know as the Logos of revelation, and whom Paul knows as the Crucified God. This is the Crucified God whose own prior proclamation and parabolic enactment celebrated the actual advent of the Kingdom of God, an advent essentially and necessarily inseparable from the end of the world, an end actually realized in the unique and actual death of I AM. That is the end which forecloses the possibility of return, and finally forecloses the possibility of eternal return, a return finally and absolutely ended in the once-and-for-all and irreversible event of the death of I AM. But if the movement of return is ended, and with it the very possibility of recovering a past moment of time, that is precisely that ending which is the beginning of a totally forward movement, and the beginning of a totally forward movement in the actuality of history. Only now is history fully born as a totally forward movement and process, and born not simply as the consequence of the death of I AM, but born in that very death, a death fully and finally reversing the movement of eternal return. The death of the Crucified God is the death of the totality of the past, just as the door of the death of I AM is a door opening only to the radical newness of the future, a future which now and for the first time is liberated from every shadow and echo of the past.

For the death of I AM is the full advent of apocalypse, that very apocalypse which Jesus celebrated and proclaimed as the Kingdom of God, and if that Kingdom dawns in parabolic enactment and eschatological proclamation, it is fully realized in the definitive and final ending of world itself, or of that world which is an embodiment of "it was," that world which is world itself and no other, that world which is not and cannot be the new creation. The power of that world is now ended, and its actuality as well, and ended in the death of its deepest ground, a ground apart from which it can only be sheer absence or nothingness, a nothingness which now and for the first time can be named as Satan. Finally, the past itself is now sheer nothingness, and this is that nothingness which alone releases the totality of the future, a future which becomes actually present in a total transformation of history. Yet that transformation is inseparable from the end of the world, the end of the world of the past, yes, but also the end of every ground in the past, of every ground of "it was," of every ground of what even faith can know as the old or original creation. Nothing less than such an ending can actually realize apocalypse, for the full advent of apocalypse is the full ending of everything which was named and known on the other side of apoclaypse, and above all the ending of the deepest ground and source of that other side. So it is by an inevitable necessity that that ending can only be known and named as the death of I AM.

True apocalypse is inevitably the reversal of everything which can be known and envisioned as past and primordial, hence it is the opposite of everything which an archaic consciousness could know as heaven, just as it is the opposite of everything which is present in and as memory or tradition, and of everything which can actually be recovered by remembrance or recall. Now the "Ancient One" quite simply is Satan, just as the "old religion" is demonism, a demonism which now can be known as an openness to the primordial and the past. Indeed, it is only now that true demonism becomes possible, for only now is an actual absence manifest and real, an absence which is the new nothingness of the past, and the very emptiness of that nothingness is not only the sign but the very seal of the abyss, and of a new abyss, an abyss which dawns only with the absolute negation of the past. That is an abyss which also makes possible the irresistible power of a new future, for a truly new and overwhelming consciousness of Hell is also an inevitable consequence of an absolute negation of the primordial and the past, for only now does the final movement of absolute negation become manifest and actual in consciousness, and the sheer awareness of absolute negation in its naked form becomes manifest as Hell. That awareness arouses a deep and ultimate energy, and an energy that can be and is released in the world, and released so as to drive forward an ultimate movement. If a consciousness of eternal damnation is only born with Christianity, and only made possible by apocalypticism, that is a consciousness which inevitably undergoes a profound uprooting, and an uprooting which is necessary and essential to a radical openness to the future.

Now even if apocalypticism was ever more fully negated and reversed in the evolution of the Christian Church, it nevertheless ever remained a deep if hidden ground in Christianity, and not only did it arise again and again, although now in subversive forms in Christian mysticism and Christian apocalypticism, but it ever remains at the center of all that Christianity which gives itself to an absolute negation of the world. Such negation was original to Christianity, although it would be reborn in Islam, and Christianity is the only religion in the world which established and realized itself by engaging in an ultimate conflict with an advanced culture and civilization, for the Roman Empire was the most powerful empire in history. If Christianity won that conflict, it did so only by releasing a new and ultimate energy, and an energy transforming consciousness itself, as consciousness now for the first time can know itself as self-consciousness and as will. Nothing is more revealing of the evolution of this consciousness than the self-realization of will and self-consciousness, and if self-consciousness and will had never previously appeared as such in history, now they are born with an irrevocable finality, and a finality inseparable from a negation of earlier forms of consciousness. The very advent of the consciousness of an individual will which is a free and personal will is a decisive sign of the negation of the density of "it was," for a negation of the finality of the past makes possible the birth of a new present, and a present which now for the first time is open to the possibility of a free and individual choice of the future.

Of course, that choice is free and necessary at once, hence the overwhelming importance of the Pauline and Augustinian understanding of predestination, but nevertheless it is an ultimate choice, and it embodies an absolute responsibility, an absolute responsibility which is an individual and personal responsibility which must necessarily and inevitably culminate in either damnation or salvation. That each and every individual has eternally been predestined either to salvation or to damnation is an inescapable consequence of such absolute responsibility, for now a uniquely individual choice for the first time becomes an absolute choice, and the overwhelming burden of that choice breaks the individual will, a breakage which is a self-negation of individual power and authority, and an ultimate self-negation inevitably leading to the realization that there is no true power or authority in the will. Then that will must know itself to be predestined, but it does so only as a free and active will, a free will which breaks itself in its own ultimate act of willing, and only that breakage makes predestination manifest, a manifestation and a self-manifestation which is inseparable from a free and ultimate act of the will. That act is the birth not only of a new willing, a willing which now must inevitably negate itself, but also of an actual willing, a willing which wills in the actuality of the present, and therein and thereby realizes a new present which is the consequence of the free and active will.

That new present is not the pure present discovered and realized in the highest moments of the ancient world, but a present which is a precarious present, a present without deep ground, but rather a present which is known and realized to be immediately moving into its own nonbeing or nothingness, a nothingness which is its own, and is its own precisely as a present and actual moment of time. The Augustinian discovery of the pure contingency of time is simultaneously a discovery of the pure contingency of the will, a will which wills and purely wills in a present moment of time, but that willing as willing is a willing of self-negation, a self-negation embodying the self-negation of time itself, and embodying that self-negation because willing inevitably occurs in an actual and present moment of time, a time which necessarily must perish in its own actualization. So as opposed to every horizon of time in the ancient world, although fully foreshadowed by Israel, a Christian time is an absolutely contingent time, for it is a time which is a consequence of an absolute negation, a time which for the first time in Western history is absolutely groundless. Only that groundlessness made possible the discovery and realization of the individual will, and a will which is an individual will precisely because it is an empty will, a will emptied of everything whatsoever which could be truly or actually present as its own.

So it is that the new "I" of the Christian consciousness is an inevitable consequence of the self-negation of I AM, for it is an "I" which is absolutely groundless, but nevertheless it is real and actual precisely in that groundlessness, a groundlessness making possible for the first time in history a self-realization of consciousness and will. For that self-realization is and only can be a self-negation, a self-negation realizing absolute self-negation and realizing it in a full and actual moment of time. That time is an absolutely contingent present, but only an absolutely contingent moment is fully and actually open to the future, a future which is a truly new future precisely because it arises out of the absolute groundlessness of the present. Now even if it took more than a millennium for Christianity itself to realize such a radically new future, that realization did occur, and it ushered in a revolutionary transformation of the totality of history. That transformation is inseparable from its ground in an absolute negation of the past, and an absolute negation of the past truly and actually realizing itself in the present, a present which now and for the first time becomes an absolute moment of self-negation. That moment of pure or absolute self-negation is a realization and the self-realization of the absolute self-negation of I AM, an absolute self-negation which is the origin and the sole origin of apocalypse.

The revolutionary and world-transforming moments of Western and Christian history are apocalyptic moments, and they embody not only ever deeper and ever more comprehensive negations of the past, but also an ever deeper and ever more universal willing of the future, a willing that is ever more deeply and ever more comprehensively an absolute will, and a will that evolves only by fully and absolutely negating itself. So it is that fully apocalyptic moments in history are fully self-negating moments, and it is precisely the actuality of such self-negation which is the driving energy of the totally forward movement of history. If this is a Faustian energy and will, it is thereby a will that can never rest or find fulfillment in the present, for it is a will that is a wholly active and actual will, and therefore a will whose very willing never ceases. Consequently, this is a will and this is a willing which could have no possible actual goal, no goal which actually could be realized, no end which is susceptible of an actual realization. Thus an apocalyptic goal is an absolute goal and it is precisely as such that it calls forth an absolute will and willing, a willing that must ever go beyond and go against itself, and therefore a will which is an absolutely negative will, a will which is absolutely directed against itself. Here, will itself is the self-willing of death, or the self-willing of the death or negation of everything whatsoever which is present and actual as its own.

So it is that absolute will is a full resolution of that new "I" that was born with the advent of the Christian consciousness. Already in Paul this new "I" or self-consciousness is a totally guilty or negative consciousness, a guilt which is ontologically understood by Augustine as privation or nothingness, but nevertheless a nothingness which is the full and individual willing of the fallen will, a will that in willing only itself in fact embodies the negation of itself, a self-negation which can never cease so long as the fallen will remains itself. For the fallen will wills to be the sole source itself, and it is just this wholly solitary will which finally can will only nothingness and nothingness alone, a nothingness which is its own identity as an absolutely solitary or absolutely sinful will, but a nothingness or guilt which nevertheless becomes present and actual when we become aware of our guilty will. That awareness can and does drive us ever more deeply into guilt, a guilt which is nothingness and a nothingness impelling the full actualization of the bad conscience, and a bad conscience arousing an ultimate revulsion against ourselves. That bad conscience drives us further and further against ourselves, but therein it ever more fully embodies the activity of the will, a will ever deepening the willing of its own nothingness, and that will as a fully actual will is a fully negative will, and a negative will which in willing itself necessarily wills against itself.

Absolute will is an absolute willing against itself, against itself as a real and actual presence, and against itself insofar as its own will is its own presence. This is the presence that must be wholly uprooted and reversed to actualize an absolute will, a will that is absolute only by being absolutely against itself. That is the pure self-negation which realizes a shattering of every present which is its own, as the absolute contingency or emptiness of time now becomes manifest and actual as the absolutely self-negating will, a will whose realization realized the Reformation, and therein realized the birth of a world that is totally turned against itself. This is the world that generates a totally negative energy, an energy most purely envisioned in the Satan of *Paradise Lost*, and an energy whose full actualization can never be stilled or calmed. But it is the impossibility of calm or rest which impels the absolute willing of the absolute will, a will that is an apocalyptic will, and is an apocalyptic will by being absolutely directed against itself. Yet that pure self-negation is also and even thereby a turn toward the future, and toward an absolute future, a future wholly other than the present, and a future which is released by an absolute turn against the present. Thus this is a future which is a fully apocalyptic future, and a fully apocalyptic future which is the final releasement of the totality of history itself.

That final releasement now occurs in the actual advent of the total self-embodiment of I AM, a self-embodiment which is not only a self-negation of the totality of the past, but a self-reversal of that totality, a self-reversal which is historically actual in the French Revolution, and interiorly actual in the new and radical realization that *God Himself is dead*. These primal words of Hegel are not only a resaying of a Lutheran hymn, but a resaying which is a Christian response to the French Revolution, and therewith a Christian response to the full and final historical actualization of apocalypse. Now death is both more actual and more universal than it had ever been before, a death ushering in a comprehensive reversal of the totality of the past, and a death which is now fully actual at the center of self-consciousness. If this death had originally been known by Paul as the death of that old Adam who is I myself, that death had also been known by Paul as an apocalyptic ending of the old creation, an ending which is itself the advent of self-consciousness, and the advent therewith of a consciousness and an actuality which is guilt and death itself. Now that self-consciousness becomes ever more fully and finally a universal consciousness, and a universal consciousness which is the self-embodiment of death, a death which is now inseparable and indistinguishable from the actuality of self-consciousness itself. And that actuality not only knows itself as death, but knows death itself as the death of God.

For to know death itself as the death of God is not only to know the finality of death, but also the ultimacy of death, an ultimacy wherein death is an ultimate event, and an ultimate event whose full actualization can only be a total presence. That total presence is an apocalyptic presence, and an apocalyptic presence of the totality of history, a totality whose final releasement occurs in the pure actuality of death itself. That actuality is a universal embodiment of the death of God, a death which is actual in every actual expression of self-consciousness, and which is equally actual in the advent of a new universal history. If the French Revolution was the first universal historical event, the first actual historical event which was destined to transform world history, and to transform world history by realizing a universal history, then this was also that event which actually ushered in a universal consciousness, and a universal consciousness which turned the world upside-down. Once the French Revolution has occurred, and has been historically realized thereafter throughout the world, then a universal history is actually established, and finally established as an irrevocable and irreversible actuality. But that universal history is actual and real only as the consequence of the death of an old world, or, rather, the death of all those worlds which are premodern and preuniversal worlds.

So it is that the actual advent of a universal history is inseparable from the full and final advent of the self-realization of death, as death now passes into the very center of the will, and the absolute self-negation of absolute will now realizes the true finality of history. That finality is inevitably a universal finality, but it realizes an actual finality only by way of the self-realization of death, and the self-realization of an ultimate death, a death that only can be the death of God. While Paul could know the death of God as the realization of apocalypse, that realization does not pass into historical actuality until the dawning of the modern world, and even if that dawning was foreseen by Dante and a host of medieval visionaries as the advent of a new world, it does not become historically actual until the English Revolution, and not historically triumphant until the French Revolution. But then it gradually but inevitably triumphs with such power as to foreclose the possibility of its annulment, and that foreclosure is a consequence of death, as the original death of the Crucified God now passes into the very center of historical actuality. And only now is the totality of history actually at hand, and at hand in the full and final actualization of ultimate death. If Paul could know that death as life, and know it by knowing the identity of crucifixion and resurrection, that death is realized in the modern world as the new life of a universal humanity.

If apocalypticism was reborn in the modern world, it was reborn in a universal form, a form negating and transcending the original biblical expressions of apocalypticism, but transcending and negating them so as to realize a universal apocalypticism. That apocalypticism is surely a fulfillment of biblical apocalypticism, and a fulfillment not only in historical actuality but also in the heights and depths of consciousness itself, a new consciousness which now ever more fully and more finally embodies the totality of history. While that totality most purely and most fully realizes itself in negative expressions of consciousness and self-consciousness, such negativity is not only a rebirth of earlier apocalypticism, but is also a genuine embodiment of a new and universal apocalypticism, an apocalypticism that Nietzsche can name as the Will to Power. Nietzsche could know the Will to Power as Eternal Recurrence, but an all-too-modern Eternal Recurrence is the very inversion of an archaic Eternal Return, and is so precisely in the very actuality of its occurrence, an occurrence which is not only totally present here and now, but whose total presence here and now is a total annulment of all other presence. While Nietzsche could name that annulment as the death of God, he could also know it as the most important event in history, for it is that event and that event alone which is the full actualization of apocalypse.

Nietzsche's Will to Power is absolute will itself, but it only becomes manifest as absolute will with the closure of every opening to transcendence, a closure effected by the event of the death of God. That event is an actual and irreversible historical event, and although it initially occurs in what Christianity knows as the Incarnation and the Crucifixion, it realizes itself in a universal expression with the full advent of modernity, an advent which is the birth of a universal humanity. But that advent is an apocalyptic advent, for it is an advent that is inseparable from the end of an old world, and it is precisely that ending that ends every ground and source of all established meaning and identity. Although a Blake could know in vision the full consequences of that ending, it only gradually realizes itself in the actualities of history, but these actualities are irrevocable and irreversible, and just as irreversible as is the voice of I AM. No one knew that irreversibility more deeply than did Nietzsche, and if that made possible the total affirmation of a new Zarathustra, the advent of that Yes-saying is inseparable from the unveiling of a total No-saying of guilt and revenge, a No-saying or *ressentiment* which is the source of everything which lies within. Then the fullness of consciousness itself could be known as the embodiment of a total No-saying, a No-saying which is the driving force or power of the totality of history.

If ancient apocalypticism initially gave birth to a full awareness of the totality of guilt and death, modern apocalypticism realizes that totality wherever there is life, for the full realization of an apocalyptic ending realizes the totality of death, a totality which now and for the first time is identical with the totality of life. So it is that it is modern apocalypticism which has realized a pure and universal negativity, a negativity which is not simply present wherever there is life, but rather a negativity that is the innermost center of life itself. Paul could know that negativity as the center of self-consciousness, just as the Fourth Gospel could know it as the darkness of the world, and Augustine could know it as the nothingness of evil, even if that nothingness is the full actuality of the fallen will. And just as the actualization of the nothingness of the will is simultaneously the first full awareness of the freedom of the will, so the modern actualization of the totality of the "bad conscience" is simultaneously the first full awareness of the advent of absolute will, a will that in the ecstatic dance of Eternal Recurrence transforms the ultimate bondage of "it was" into the ultimate freedom of "thus I willed it." Yet the ultimate freedom of Eternal Recurrence only becomes manifest and real as a consequence of an ultimate reversal of consciousness, a reversal which itself is possible only as the consequence of an actual epiphany of the totality of No-saying, a totality which is the purely negative identity of consciousness itself.

Now if an actual awareness of the forward movement of a universal history was born only with the advent of apocalypticism, a forward movement which is a progressive descent into sin and death, that forward movement can therein and thereby be known as a theodicy, a theodicy in which the "cunning of reason" realizes life through death and violence, and ecstatic joy through pain and guilt. But that is a joy and a life which is a consequence of the ending of the center of consciousness, an ending which is not only a dissolution of the active and actual subject of consciousness, but also an ending dissolving every possible ground of consciousness, with the result that consciousness now becomes not only groundless and centerless, but also a consciousness which simultaneously is and is not itself. Thereby a distinctively and uniquely Western self-consciousness is ended, and with that ending consciousness realizes a new anonymity, an anonymity in which all boundaries disappear, and in which nothing whatsoever is manifest and real which can be known and named as consciousness and consciousness alone. "Here Comes Everybody" is now the subject and center of consciousness, but that is a center which is nobody, and it is nowhere as a distinct and individual center, as a center which is and only is itself.

The depths of consciousness are now an absolutely anonymous consciousness, as these depths embody the groundlessness and the centerlessness which released them, and if now the center is everywhere and the circumference nowhere, that is because center as center has wholly disappeared and with that disappearance cosmos and chaos are one and indistinguishable. There is no more decisive expression of the dawning of the modern world than the realization of the infinity of the universe, and if this occurred with the dissolution of the Middle Ages it was fully embodied in the scientific revolution of the seventeenth century, a revolution which in Newton's *Principia* destroyed a transcendent celestial world by an ontological and mathematical realization of an infinite universe, and did so with an apocalyptic finality. That revolution was reborn in the scientific revolutions of the twentieth century, but reborn in such a way as to destroy the very possibility of a universe, as a singular or linear perspective of any kind broke down and passed into seemingly innumerable perspectives, perspectives erasing every real distinction between observer and observed, and every real distinction between here and there or center and circumference. If Newton in his *Opticks* could know an absolute space which is the boundless uniform *Sensorium* of God, that is the very space which in full modernity loses every trace or sign of a transcendent source or ground, and with that disappearance space as space is indistinguishable from chaos.

Nothing is more distinctive of full modernity or postmodernity than a full realization of absolute contingency, and if classical Christendom from Augustine through Aquinas could know real contingency as the decisive sign and seal of the absolute presence of God, contingency now becomes the very opposite of its former identity, as its full realization dissolves every distinction between contingency and necessity or order and chance. Therein and thereby the absolute presence of God passes into the absolute absence of God, and all signs and images of God, or of the gracious presence and identity of God, simply disappear from all real and

actual expressions of consciousness. Blake could inaugurate a full
modernity by naming God as Satan, a name unveiling the absolute absence or emptiness of God in the modern world, and this is
precisely the purely abstract or unreal God who dies in the full
realization of the modern consciousness. But that realization is inseparable from the epiphany of God as Satan, as absolute ground is
now absolutely groundless, and light itself is indistinguishable
from darkness, a darkness which is the pure otherness of every
given meaning and identity, an otherness that is now quite simply
existence and life. Now night falls upon all light, or upon all light
that is a reflection of the past, as an original and now absolute
chaos becomes all in all.

Ancient apocalypticism could know such a chaos as the very
destiny of the world, and know it as a destiny which is immediately at hand, and at hand in the near advent of the end of the
world. Nothing is more fundamental to genuine apocalypticism
of any kind than total ending, an ending that is the ending of
every beginning, and yet an ending which is a final and once-and-
for-all event. An irrevocable ending is a full realization of an irreversible beginning, for that beginning cannot stand alone as a
once-and-for-all event, and cannot do so if only because of the
very momentum of a real and actual beginning, a momentum
necessarily issuing in a movement which must have an end. That
necessity is simply the necessity of actuality itself, a necessity
wherein life and death are one, for the actualization of life inevitably culminates in the actualization of death, and a death which
is every bit as real as is life itself. But the actuality of death is not
simply identical with the actuality of life, indeed, it is its very opposite, and is its opposite by being the full and actual reversal of
life. While archaic symbolisms know an alpha and an omega which
are identical, apocalyptic symbolisms can only know an omega
which is the intrinsic opposite of alpha, and the intrinsic opposite
of beginning if only because an apocalyptic ending ends the very
possibility of beginning.

Both the actual meaning and the actual reality of a pure and
total opposition were only born with the advent of apocalypticism, as opposites for the first time appear and are real as pure
and total opposites, thereby releasing a violent opposition and reversal of both consciousness and history. Opposites which Paul
could know as "flesh" and Spirit or sin and grace or old aeon and
new aeon now engage in violent opposition, an opposition deriving from their identity as pure and total opposites, and from their

conjunction in a new consciousness and a new history. Now and for the first time an ultimate beginning can be known as coming to an end, and if that beginning for Paul is original sin, original sin can only be known and named as a consequence of apocalyptic ending, an ending which is the eternal death of sin. Only the realization that the ultimate and final death of sin is immediately at hand makes possible a realization of the totality of sin, a totality which is the totality of history and cosmos alike, and a totality which has finally been shattered by the crucifixion and the resurrection of Christ. If Christ is the New Adam, the totality of fall is the Old Adam, and now the Old Adam is absolutely groundless, a real and actual groundlessness which is the consequence of the actual advent of the End. For it is the actual advent of the End which is the source of the pure and total opposition between the opposites, an opposition which for the first time makes manifest and real the actuality of intrinsic and total opposition.

Only the advent of this opposition made possible an apprehension of apocalyptic ending, an ending which is the ending of everything which is given in consciousness and history, which is to say of everything which is the intrinsic otherness of the total grace of apocalypse. No true dualism is or could be present here, for the pure "isness" of total grace is not only the intrinsic opposite of sin and death, its very actualization effects the eternal death of sin and death, and now and for the first time sin and death can be known to be that pure nothingness which is their destiny. So the very presence of a pure and total opposition is only possible as the consequence of the immediate coming of the full and final ending of that opposition, an ending whose very actualization alone draws forth and makes real an actual and total opposition, and an opposition whose very totality is inseparable from its immediately coming to an end. No doubt an original and an apocalyptic Christianity could not survive beyond one or two generations, but if its ending effected the most radical transformation of a religious movement in history, that is but one sign of the power of an apocalyptic ending, an ending releasing a new and total historical energy, and an energy that was destined to transform the world.

And transform the world it did by releasing a totally forward movement of history and consciousness, for now the very possibility of a new and ultimate beginning is ended, and ended in the depths of consciousness, an ending that is the inevitable consequence of the full advent of apocalypse. Now even if the full realization of that ending did not occur until the passage of two millennia, occur it did, and that occurrence is the overwhelming reality of our own time. Whereas Paul could know an apocalyptic realization in the advent of self-consciousness, a self-consciousness which is a purely negative and self-negating consciousness, our own world knows the totality of consciousness as a purely negative and self-negating consciousness, a consciousness in which the interiority of consciousness has been reversed, and reversed in the advent of a total consciousness which is interior and exterior at once. So much is this the case that now the interior and exterior poles of consciousness are indistinguishable, and just as indistinguishable as are the center and the circumference of space. Yet if center itself is now centerless, that is precisely the centerlessness releasing a new totality, a totality of consciousness and cosmos alike, and even if this totality is a rebirth of archaic visions of totality, now and for the first time totality itself is both fully actual and fully at hand.

The very epiphany of a new and actual totality has ended that very history and consciousness which is its source, an ending which is a new and final beginning of the ending of consciousness and history, an ending which is present now as it has never been present before. If our history was born by way of a forward and ever more total movement of consciousness, now it is ending in the dissolution of that movement, a dissolution which is the dissolution of death. Nothing was more characteristic of the advent of modernity than the dominant power of the idea and the symbol of progress, and nothing is more characteristic of the advent of postmodernity than the erosion and erasure of the very possibility of any kind of deep or genuine progress, except insofar as real and existing possibilities will become ever more universal throughout the world. For the forward movement of consciousness has reached its terminus, or reached its terminus in terms of the closure of possibilities of realizing truly new vistas and horizons or new horizons and vistas realizing a truly and deeply evolutionary movement of consciousness. The revolutionary thinkers of the nineteenth century all knew the inevitable necessity of such closure, and knew it at the center of their deepest thinking, just as the revolutionary imagination of the twentieth century has again and again realized such closure in its deepest expressions, expressions which themselves have ended the actual possibility of a forward movement of the imagination.

Yet an absolute beginning remains at hand, a once-and-for-all beginning which is present not only in our cosmologies, but present also in our apprehension of the very identity of consciousness. For it is impossible for us even to entertain the possibility of an eternal consciousness, a consciousness that did not actually begin and evolve. If consciousness is itself only as the consequence of a real and actual beginning, it also is itself only as the consequence of a real and actual ending. That ending can only be symmetrical with its own beginning, hence it must be every bit as actual as is the actuality of beginning, and every bit as final as is the finality of beginning. No possibility of eternal life lies here at hand, no actual possibility of the eternity of either cosmos or consciousness. For the evolutionary expansion of both cosmos and consciousness must come to an end, and inevitably come to an end, an ending which is quite simply the end of life. That ending is all that we can actually know as grace, and actually know as the total grace of apocalypse, a grace which is eternal death. But that grace, too, is a consequence of beginning, and of an irrevocable and irreversible beginning, a once-and-for-all beginning which is the source of actuality, and the source of that actuality which is the sole arena of an apocalyptic grace.

If an apocalyptic grace is a total grace, and a grace embodying a new totality, the advent of that totality is inseparable from an apocalyptic ending, an ending which itself is total and which comprehends all that totality which is other than apocalypse. Accordingly, to know an apocalyptic ending is to know and to realize apocalypse itself, and the depth and comprehensiveness of that ending embodies the power and the totality of the apocalypse which is present, and present precisely in that very ending. Now death itself embodies an actuality that never previously was present, and apocalyptically that death may be named as life, a life of total grace, but a grace that is actually present only through death. If Christianity originally knew the advent of the totality of death, world itself now knows the full totality of death, and if this is a real and actual totality, then that totality can apocalyptically be named as a totality of grace. But it can be so named only if it is known and realized as the totality of death, a death that now is all in all, or all in all insofar as it is actually and totally present. Now an apocalyptic grace is everywhere, and it is everywhere present as death, a death or emptiness which is a total presence, and a total presence which is actuality itself.

Nothing is more evasive of that totality than is an affirmation of life and of life alone, unless it be an affirmation of God and of God alone, a God who is the God of life and not of death, a God who is and who only is eternal life. But that is an affirmation which has ceased to be present in either our imaginative or our conceptual language, and that cessation is a culmination of two millennia of our history, a culmination which can be nothing less than the ending of our history itself. Now even if the ending of our history is simultaneously the advent of a universal history, there is nothing in that advent which lessens the impact of death, the death of all and of everything which Christendom has known as life. And that Christendom that ended with the French Revolution is not simply and only a premodern Western history, but rather the totality of history as present and actual to a center and subject of consciousness, and above all the totality of history as grounded in a transcendent subject and center, a center which Christendom knew and named as God. That is the God who died with the full actualization of modernity, but that death is not only the death of a transcendent center, it is the death of any and every center of consciousness, and of any and every center of history. So it is that the advent of an actual centerlessness is the advent of an actual universality, but that universality is possible and actual only through death, the death of every possible center of history or consciousness, and hence the death of every consciousness and history which could possibly be our own.

That is why the advent of a total anonymity is inseparable from the advent of an actual universality, for that universality brings an end to every previous center of identity, and thereby brings an end to every center which is center and center alone. Now this is a real and actual ending, and an actual ending which is an apocalyptic and universal ending, and therefore the ending of every beginning which we can know and realize as a real and actual beginning. So it is that everything which we have known and named as life is now ending, and ending with an irreversible and irrevocable finality, a finality that we can resist only by evading the actuality of our ending itself. But even that evasion is now becoming ever more futile and impossible, and impossible because every beginning which we can actually know is the beginning of a final ending, an ending in which there cannot possibly be a new beginning. A new beginning is just that which is impossible for us, and impossible because of the actual and the total presence of apocalyptic grace, a grace that interiorly can be known and named only as death, a death consuming every center which is our own, and a death eroding every movement which we have known and named as life. For not only is every actual beginning now ending, but therewith beginning itself is ending, and ending as a new beginning.

Now there is nothing which is not actually present, and that ultimate absence forecloses the possibility of an actual beginning, the beginning of anything which is not present here and now. Ours is an ending which can never begin again, or begin again as a new ending, an ending which is not present now. For ours is an ending which is a total ending, an ending which is apocalypse, yes, and an apocalypse which can never be repeated or renewed. It is the very essence of apocalypse that is a once-and-for-all event, an event that is a total event, and therefore an event that can never occur again. For an apocalyptic eternal recurrence is not an archaic eternal return, and is not eternal return because it occurs totally here and now, a here and now which is the finality of actuality itself. That finality can never begin again, or begin in the actuality of a future that is new, a future that is not present here and now, or a future lying outside of the totality of an apocalyptic present. A totally apocalyptic present is inevitably the ending of both the future and the past, the ending of every past that can be known as "it was," and the ending of every future that can be known or can be realized as "it will be." Now there can be neither a return of the past nor a coming of the future, or not a coming or a return which is not wholly and totally present here and now.

Even in its initial beginning an apocalyptic symbolism could know the nothingness of sin, death, and Satan, a nothingness that is the consequence of an apocalyptic ending, and a nothingness that is the real and intrinsic opposite of a new creation. This is a nothingness which Augustine understood as the guilty or sinful will, a will that is actual in its evil or nothingness, but nevertheless an absolutely empty will, a will that is only insofar as it is an absence or privation of being. Thus the sinful will actually is and yet ultimately is not, a dialectical polarity simultaneously releasing a new consciousness of freedom and a new consciousness of guilt, and this double or doubled consciousness is an absolutely negative consciousness which ever more gradually and comprehensively releases the full actualization of an absolutely self-negating willing and will. But that self-negation must inevitably come to an end, must necessarily come to its own fulfillment, a fulfillment or consummation which is the totality of death and nothingness. Now that nothingness no longer lies at the center of the will, it is far rather a nothingness that is all and all, and is all and all in everything whatsoever which is now manifest and actual as consciousness and history.

Augustine could know the absolute privation of the totally sinful will only by knowing the absolute "isness" of a totally gracious God, a God whose total graciousness predestines sin to an eternal death or Hell, and a total graciousness which simultaneously predestines the elect to eternal life. That predestination is one act of God, and, for Augustine, it is not a new act, and there is no new will in predestination, for God wills all that He will simultaneously, in one act, and eternally. That act of God is an enactment of the absolute love and grace of God, a grace which freely gives eternal life, and a grace which wills the eternal death of death, and there is no distinction whatsoever within the eternal act and will of God between predestination to eternal death and predestination to eternal life. Nothing is more central or more fundamental in the Christian understanding of God than is the doctrine of predestination, and it is shared by every major Christian theologian from Augustine and Aquinas through Luther and Calvin and beyond, and is imaginatively enacted in the Christian epic from Dante through Joyce. For predestination is the enactment of total grace, a grace that is freely willed in the eternal act of God, and that is actually embodied in what the Christian finally knows as an absolutely providential history. If that providential history has its actual beginning in fall, it has its actual ending in apocalypse, an apocalypse which is grounded in the *felix culpa* of the fortunate fall, a fortunate fall releasing that historical actuality which is absolutely reversed in apocalypse.

Yet the Christian God can be known to be present and actual only in that self-consciousness which is fully free and wholly guilty at once, a doubled consciousness which is both actually free and yet eternally predestined, and which deeply knows itself to be both free and enslaved at the very center of its consciousness. That self-consciousness knows God as being even more fully present than itself, and it is precisely thereby that it knows itself as both a free and an enslaved center of consciousness, and knows its deepest freedom by knowing the eternal predestination of God. For that predestination is the act of grace, and the act of grace which is simultaneously the act of creation, for creation and predestination are finally indistinguishable in the eternal act of God, an act which freely wills the totality of grace. That totality can be named as God and as God alone, or can be so named by the actuality of self-consciousness, a self-consciousness which knows itself as the image of God, and thus knows itself as the image of the total freedom and the total actuality of God.

But the actualization of a fallen consciousness knows that freedom and that actuality as a wholly negative actuality and a wholly negative will, a will and an actuality which is sin itself, and therefore is that nothingness which is only possible by way of the actual absence of God. This is an absence which becomes ever deeper and ever more comprehensive in the full realization of the fallen will, a will which in itself knows its own nothingness as the full absence of God, and as it ever more fully realizes itself it realizes that nothingness in the totality of its own acts and embodiments. But these enactments occur in an absolutely providential history, a history whose every act is finally willed by God, and eternally willed in the one and only eternal act of God. And if this is a history that culminates in the death of God, that is a death that is eternally willed by God, and actually enacted in the self-negation of I AM. If that actual self-negation inaugurates apocalypse, and inaugurates apocalypse as a once-and-for-all and irreversible and total event, that event is the final and total self-embodiment of God. But the total self-embodiment of God can only be the total self-dissolution of the actuality of God as God, a self-dissolution realizing itself in the self-negation of the fallen image of God, as center itself passes into centerlessness throughout history and consciousness, and the full actualization of the self-embodiment of God is the full actualization of apocalypse.

Now a full and final nothingness is actually at hand, and at hand in actuality itself, an actuality which is itself the total absence of the actuality of God as God, but nevertheless a full embodiment of the total grace of God. Thereby an original self-naming of God wholly passes into silence, and the ultimate speech of God is now present and actual as the silence of God, a silence embodying the total dissolution of God as God. That dissolution is a self-dissolution, and a self-dissolution which is a self-negation, a self-negation which is the consummation of the original self-negation of I AM. Now a word and a speech which originally was word and speech alone is silence and silence alone, a silence ending the actuality of divine speech, and therewith and thereby ending the actuality of all speech and of all voice which is individual and unique., If this is a new silence, and a new silence which is all in all, it is also a resolution of an original speech, a speech which was absolutely individual and absolutely unique. Now that uniqueness and individuality is reversed in a new voice which at bottom is silence itself, a voice of silence which is ever increasingly and ever finally an embodiment of nothingness, and an embodiment of that nothingness which is finally an apocalyptic and total grace.

If the final words of the Word of revelation are "It is finished," the final actuality of an apocalyptic history is a finished actuality, an actuality whose center and ground have perished. But that perishing is finally indistinguishable from absolute origin, an origin which is creation, and is predestination as well. For a once-and-for-all beginning can only be consummated in a once-and-for-all ending, an ending whose silence is a renewal of that silence prior to the beginning, but a renewal which is a reversal of the silence of a pure and total transcendence. Now silence actually speaks, it speaks through an actual voice of silence, a voice which is present here and now, but present only in the absence of the actuality of speech. That absence can only be present and real through the total presence of nothingness, a new nothingness which is a fully actual nothingness, and a fully actual nothingness because it is actuality itself. That actuality is the actuality of God, but now the actuality of the total presence of the self-embodiment of God, a self-embodiment which is the self-negation of I AM. That God whom Paul could know as the God who will be all in all, is all in all in apocalypse, an apocalypse in which God and nothingness are one. Now the center is everywhere, and it is actually everywhere, but thereby the center is nowhere, a nowhere in which center and periphery or center and nothingness are actually one.

Silence is the one grace that remains real and actual to us, and it is real as it has never been before, and is so if only because of its silencing of every other source of grace. The very totality of the silence now engulfing us is necessarily a totality of death, but the totality of death is inevitably the totality of nothingness, a totality which is a reversal and an absolute reversal of what the Christian once knew as the creation. That creation has long since disappeared from view, and disappeared in the wake of the death of the Creator, a death finally ending every positive and ultimate ground. Now the actuality of both space and time is a silent actuality, a silence in which voice as voice is absent, and in that absence voice itself is silence. But it is an actual silence, an actuality in which silence is overwhelmingly present, and overwhelmingly present as a center which is center and periphery at once. If that silence is the silence of death, it is the silence of the totality of death, a totality finally ending the very possibility of the actuality of speech. And this is grace, the deepest grace that could be present to us, and the only grace that could be real to us.

And it is real to us, and real as an apocalyptic grace, an apocalyptic grace which is the grace of ending itself. If Christendom could know grace as the grace of beginning, and the grace of absolute beginning, we can know grace as the grace of absolute ending, and know it only by the final loss of the grace of beginning. Only that loss makes possible the grace of ending, for ending is the ending of beginning, and absolute ending is the absolute ending of beginning. And if beginning begins as "God said," ending begins, and absolutely begins, as God's silence, a silence which is wholly other than that silence which was prior to beginning, and wholly other because it is a silence that can never be ended. For if beginning as beginning is a once-and-for-all and irreversible event, ending as ending is equally so such an absolute and irreversible event, and is so precisely as ending. So it is that the silence of God is as fully real as is the revelation of God, indeed, it is that revelation, but it is that revelation as the revelation of ending, an ending which is the reversal of beginning, and the absolute reversal of an absolute beginning. And that reversal is as fully and as totally gracious as is absolute beginning, and is so as the very fulfillment of that beginning.

Yes, it is finished, and it is finished for all which has irretrievably begun, for all which is actual and here and now. "Being begins in every now," but it begins in every now only because it ends in every now, only because of the ultimacy of ending itself, an ending which as ending is now all in all. Only when beginning has ended as beginning does it fulfill itself, and it fulfills itself in its own consummation, a consummation in which "God said" has wholly and finally passed into silence. If that silence is the silence of death, it is the silence of eternal death, and thus it is a silence which can never be spoken. And a silence that can never be spoken is the very opposite of that silence which was the site of our once-and-for-all beginning, and is the real and actual opposite of that silence because it is a final silence, a silence finally foreclosing the possibility of speech. If there is a *coincidentia oppositorum* between absolute beginning and absolute ending, it lies wholly in the once-and-for-all finality of each event, and if each finality is the opposite of the other, each is also necessary and essential to the other, for an actual beginning must finally end, just as an actual ending is an ending of an actual beginning. And if only an absolute grace could make possible and actual an absolute beginning, only an absolute grace could make possible and actual an absolute ending.

While that grace can be known as apocalyptic grace, and even can be named as the apocalypse of God, it can be so known only through death, and only through eternal death, an eternal death which is a final ending. If grace is everywhere, and is everywhere here and now, it is everywhere as death and nothingness, and finally as the death and nothingness of I AM. Our deepest seers have known such nothingness as grace, and so known it both in the ancient and the modern worlds, for at no other point is there a deeper coincidence between the postmodern and the ancient worlds. But now such grace is actually and historically present, and present in the final ending of history, an ending which is not only the ending of every center of consciousness, but also and even therefore the ending of horizon or world. If this is resurrection, it is the resurrection of eternal death, a resurrection which is crucifixion, but it is only as crucifixion that it is actually manifest and real. Indeed, apocalyptic ending can itself be known as the apocalypse of God, and the apocalypse of the Crucified God, as the death of the Crucified God is now universally realized as a final and total event. But it is universally realized as eternal death, an eternal death which is now actuality itself, and an actuality which is the total realization of the Crucified God.

Yet the total realization of the Crucified God is the final actualization of the silence of God, that silence is nothingness and nothingness alone, but a new nothingness, a nothingness which is the fullness and the finality of historical actuality. Now the resurrection of the dead is actually present, and universally present in the consummation of history, a consummation which is the apotheosis of death itself. That apotheosis is resurrection, and the resurrection of eternal death, an eternal death that is the total silence of God. If that silence dawned with the proclamation and parabolic enactment of the Kingdom of God, it is consummated in the apocalypse of God, an apocalypse that is finally and only the totality of silence. That silence is absolute grace, and the absolute grace of the apocalypse of God, an apocalypse that is the new totality of absolute ending. And if that totality is as absolutely new as is the once-and-for-all event of absolute beginning, it is not only the ending of that beginning, but the ending of every beginning, the ending of everything except ending itself. Now ending is all, and ending is everywhere, and everywhere where the echoes of speech and presence are actual and real. But those echoes are echoes and only echoes, and echoes dissolving in a new plenitude of silence, a silence which is the silence of God.

ROBERT P. SCHARLEMANN

5
———

A RESPONSE

IT WILL be clear to readers of the preceding essays that they do not fit cleanly under a single identifying label. But they have enough interests in common and enough divergences to warrant trying to turn them into a three-way conversation by further questions. In all three essays there is an intertwining of two references to the end. The one is to the end of the twentieth century and to the possible significance of that end for theology (or, alternatively, of theology for that coming to an end of a chronological period); the other reference is to the end eschatologically, that is, to the question of how to think of the end absolutely, or of the end as end— not the end of this or that but just the end. All three authors seem to affirm that the intellectual or spiritual situation at the end of the twentieth century can be characterized by the end of ontotheology or, in more specifically Heideggerian terms, the end of the metaphysical epoch in the thinking of being. "Metaphysics" in this case refers to a way of thinking in which the difference between being as such (*Sein*) and being as a being (*Seiendes*) does not become a theme at all; it does not occur to anyone to think about that difference. Not thinking of that difference is what makes possible an equation of "God" with "being," for God can then be thought of as a supreme being which is, indiscriminately, over all other beings and in all other beings. At this point we do not need to go into the extent to which Heidegger's characterization applies to theologians in this tradition—they were never the object of Heidegger's attention—as it does to the philosophers. For, regardless of its epochal or historical application, the theme of the end of metaphysics and ontotheology has become current in its own right today. The assertion of such an end sets the background for Winquist's as well as Taylor's theological proposal. It does so in Altizer's case too, although in a somewhat different way; for there seems to me to be in Altizer, despite the frequent appeals to Hegel, a continuation of a kind of Protestant biblical theology that uses a certain philosophical language but is fundamentally indifferent to metaphysical or philosophical questions in themselves.

What Is the End?

Let me begin by selecting a theme on which there appears to be a great difference, in this case between Taylor and Altizer. Taylor formulates a difference between the end as apocalypse and the end as disaster, and he takes issue with Altizer's conception of the end as total presence. What is under question is the structure or the significance of the end as such.

Taylor challenges Altizer's conception of the end as apocalypse, or total presence, in favor of an end conceived as "disaster." He does so, if I am not mistaken, on intrinsic and phenomenological grounds. By that I mean he does not simply offer a different reading of historical or other material data. Rather, by way of Blanchot, he calls attention to a feature of the end that appears in an existential phenomenology. He points out the peculiarity that the end, existentially grasped as my-death, never comes; it is always in the coming but never gets here. (I use the hyphenated *my-death* to mean death in this existential sense of what "I," that is, anyone in the first person singular, can do or what can happen to "me.") In that connection, he also seems to agree with Blanchot in calling into question whether death can be, as Heidegger's analysis in *Being and Time* indicates it to be, the authentic phenomenon par excellence, the phenomenon that most distinguishes the self in its propriety, its own I-ness or *Eigentlichkeit*. He concludes that, contrary to the contention that at the end there is total presence, the end is not apocalypse but disaster, not the fulfillment but the dispersal of the self as a self on its own. These seem to be clearly opposed views of the end as end, and the opposition, when seen from the point of view of Taylor's objection to the notion of the end as total presence, is based upon alternate conceptions of what is even possible as the end.

With this brief résumé of the difference, I want to put a question to each of the two. Either Taylor or Altizer, or both of them, may wish to disagree with this account of the difference. That itself would shed additional light on the question. But on the assumption that this résumé does formulate a statement of the difference between them, there are some questions to be posed.

What Taylor suggests about the futurity (the adventivity, or *Zukünftigkeit*) of the existential end (my-death) is clearly true. The end is by its very nature always in the coming but never getting here (for "me"). But I wonder whether this is really an objection to the connection between death and the propriety of the self as I. Does it really undermine the contention, familiar to us since Heidegger's analysis in *Being and Time*, that death is the possibility most my *own?* It does not seem to me to do so unless one overlooks the difference between possibility and actuality. Taylor observes that death can never really come because, although it is always a possibility, it is not a possibility for "me." When death comes, it is not an event in "my" world, not an event for "me" any longer. It is on that basis that he argues against the very possibility of the end as total presence. But, granted that "my" death is never an event for "me," it does not seem to follow, as Taylor suggests, that death is not connected with the propriety of the self, or the self's being a self as an I. For the point being made when it is said that death is the possibility most my own—the possibility that most reveals the *Eigentlichkeit* of the self—is that death is the end that I, as a subject in the first person singular, always (only) *can* do but never *do* do. The connection between the phenomenon of the end and the phenomenon of the propriety of the I is one of sheer *possibility*. With respect to other possibilities, an "I can" can be turned into an "I do": "I can listen to the radio" of moment t can be turned into "I do listen to the radio" of moment t'; "N can die" of today can become "N died" of some future day. The only "I can" which can never be converted into a corresponding "I do" is the "I can" of "I can die." Hence, while it is true that my-death never arrives as an event for me, this does not sever the connection between authenticity and possibility in that phenomenon; on the contrary, it confirms the connection. The event which reveals the I-ness of the I in relation to its pure possibility (its "I can"), the event which is the possibility most my own, is the end meant in the thought "I can die."[1] It is the only possibility that can never be turned into an actuality and the only possibility that can never be referred in its purity as a possibility to anyone other than the self in the form of "I." The phenomenon of the end as death is such that only I, and I alone, always "can" do but never "do" do it.

If, then, the connection between death and the propriety of the self (or the self's being an I in isolated singularity) is, contrary to the view that Blanchot has expressed, the most intimate one, does it not follow that the end at least *can* be, if not that it *must* be, "apocalypse" instead of "disaster"? If so, then a phenomenology of my-death will not decide between the two outcomes. The self comes into its own as an I when faced with the phenomenon of death, and it comes into its own in the sphere of the "I can" (possibility). It *does* come into its own; so there is an actuality, a fulfillment about it. But it comes into its own in the anticipation of the possibility that is most its own, the possibility "my death."

Thus my question to Taylor and Altizer has two sides to it. On the one side is this set of questions: What is the nature of the combination of the fulfillment and the possibility? In what sense is the combination a disaster or a total presence? And in what conceptual frame of reference do the concepts of disaster and apocalypse constitute alternatives? "Disaster" (ill-starred fortune) and "apocalypse" (revealing the hidden) would not normally come to mind as alternative possibilities. What is it that links them together as reciprocally exclusive? The other side of the question involves the basis on which an answer can be given. Altizer's account is a portrait of the historical movement toward apocalypse or total presence; it is not a reflection on the phenomenological meaning of end. History, theologically understood, is in this account the movement in which God gives up transcendence and becomes fully present; it is the movement in which God gives up being deity. It has the nature of a *kenosis*, a self-emptying or self-divesting of deity, so that it can be given the title of the death of God. This history begins with the disclosure of the divine name in the voice that comes to Moses from the burning bush "I Am Who I Am," and it ends with the crucifixion of Jesus where the voice of any transcendent "I Am" is completely silent. But that silence is also a resurrection in that it represents a total presence, the presence in *any* "I am" of what first appeared in a special disclosure. "Total presence" designates the end of the theological history that begins with the self-naming of God. The end occurs in principle with the death of Jesus but is not turned into actuality until Christendom's negation of the occurrence is in turn negated (as in Joyce's *Ulysses*).

The notion of total presence I take to be related both to that of absolute consciousness in Hegel's phenomenology and to that of omnipresence in scholastic theology. Total presence is the self-negation of eternal and transcendent presence. But how is total presence different from those related concepts? Or what is the route by which one arrives at the concept of total presence? If Psalm 139 is read as the psalmist's account of the experience of divine omnipresence, can one find a similar account of the experience of total presence? Total presence is to mean that there is no longer a difference between what is so and what should be so—that there is a complete reconciliation with destiny or history, with the unalterable "It was," instead of the disconsolate state of resentment portrayed by Nietzsche. It seems also to mean that there is no distinction between the "I am" of anyone and the "I am" that is the fully immanent form of the "I am" that was the self-disclosure of the name of God. Is there a portrait of the experience of total presence comparable to the portrait of the experience of omnipresence in Psalm 139? In that psalm we find a poetic expression of the experience of omnipresence. Where do we find a comparable expression of the experience of total presence? Taylor suggests this kind of reconciliation or harmony, which was impossible in Hegel of the nineteenth century, not only may not have become actual toward the end of the twentieth but may not even be possible. Is that the case?

A more general question, but one still related to the theme of how Altizer's concepts are related to those of the theological tradition, is the question why the whole of history seems to be given the title of the "death" of God? This seems to cancel the temporality of history. History may be the scene of unrepeatable events, but it is told in the form of "this happened and then something else happened" (even if the telling is, as Barth said with Calvin, only the monotonous repetition of the story of human folly and divine providence). But if everything that was distinguished in theology by reference to the distinct events of incarnation, crucifixion, and resurrection is subsumed under the title of the death of God, what becomes of the temporal sequence, the real occurring, of this history? One answer might be to deconstruct the theism in Altizer's theology. The frame of reference of his theology is still a theistic metaphysics. Only within such a metaphysics can the concepts of transcendence and immanence (presence) be the basic ones they are in Altizer's theology, in which the *kenosis* of deity is put in terms of the death of the transcendent

God. Yet this very theism is denied by the way in which the distinctions essential to it are collapsed into the one event called the death (which is also the resurrection) of God. (Is that likewise the reason why Paul's proclamation of "Christ and him crucified" is said to be a proclamation of "the crucified *God*"?) When Tertullian spoke of the death of God, he did so in the context of the question whether one can say that in the death of Jesus it was not only the humanity but also the divinity in Jesus that died. That was the context of the debates about the death of God in Protestant orthodoxy too. In these cases, however, the distinction between incarnation and crucifixion was not erased. That a metaphysical theism is being denied from within metaphysical theism is one possible answer to the question of why in Altizer's theology the distinctions are collapsed. But since this explanation suggests a more calculated strategy than what appears in his writings, it is a question I shall use this occasion to pose to Altizer.

When does the end occur? In Hegel's history of spirit, there was a "speculative Good Friday," a point in the development of philosophical thought at which the outward events of Christian history, expressed in objective images (*Vortstellungen*), are recapitulated within thought itself. Critical philosophy repeats, purely within the sphere of thought, the crucifixion of incarnate deity. It does so because the standpoint of critical philosophy is that of the autonomous ego; critical philosophy is that form of thought in which the standpoint and agent of all judgment are those of the I as such. Anything that purports to displace judgment from its rooting in the I as such as to be condemned. With this "speculative Good Friday," the externality of the crucifixion of Jesus is completely internalized, and critical thinking is itself nothing else than the philosophical recapitulation of that Good Friday. That speculative thinking then arises out of critical thinking is, similarly, the recurrence in thought of the event which the disciples of Jesus reported as his resurrection. Such a conception animates Altizer's theological reading of history as well. He charts it, however, not by reference to philosophical history but by reference to works of art. Dante, Milton, Blake, Joyce, and the like are the bearers and interpreters of the movement toward the end of history. One of the costs of doing this is that the choice of events seems more arbitrary than either the biblical history or the speculative extension of that history. What, for example, makes the French Revolution rather than, say, Greek philosophy or the religious tolerance of Frederick II of Sicily (the "first modern man," as Burkhardt called him) the "first universal event"? Have I overlooked something in seeking a rationale in the choices?

In any case, if for both Taylor and Altizer the twentieth century is the end of an epoch, there still appears to be a difference in the way Taylor's theology (a/theology) aligns the three concepts of being, nothing, and God and the way Altizer's does. Both the concept of a/theology and his remarks about nothingness suggest that Taylor conceives of nothingness as beyond both being and God. What is not clear is whether this is meant to apply only to a theistic conception of God. If God is, theistically, equated with supreme being, from which all elements of nonbeing are excluded, then nothingness—neither being nor nonbeing, and both being and nonbeing—is the more original concept. This seems to me to be the position that Taylor represents, and it may be one of the reasons why the question of the self plays a prominent role in his works whereas it appears hardly at all in Altizer's. Altizer, on the other hand, aligns the concepts in such a way that God is beyond both being and nothing. Apocalypse is, therefore, the unveiling of God, and total presence is the presence of God. This remains true even if God who is thus present is not present as "transcendent" deity but as the death of transcendent deity or, as Schelling might have put it, the end of mythology. Could one do a phenomenological analysis of the death of God comparable to a Heideggerian reflection on the "I can die"? If, for the self, death is the *possibility* most my own (and a possibility never convertible to an actuality), is this same phenomenon of death the *actuality* most God's own (and an actuality with never an antecedent possibility)? Does the event which appears for "me" always in the form of "I can always," that is, as the possibility most my own, also appear as the actuality most other than mine, that is, in the form of "God can never"? If so, would it show the same phenomenon as the one indicated in Altizer's wording: "To know death itself as the death of God is not only to know the finality of death but also the ultimacy of death, . . . an ultimate event whose full actualization can only be total presence"?

If my reading of the difference between Taylor and Altizer is correct, then Altizer's is a more traditionally Christian and Taylor's a more "Buddhist" version of the same. Altizer does speak of Christian theology as having to be reborn by an immersion in Buddhism; and this provides one connection between postmodern nihilism and Christian theology in *History as Apocalypse.* But the ordering of the concepts of God and nothing seems to be different in Altizer's Christian atheism from what it is in Taylor's a/theology. So let me put the question to both: Is nothingness beyond God, or is God beyond nothingness? Or if "God and nothingness are one," how are we to think the content of the "one" differently from the content of "nothingness"? What seems clear is that, if the twentieth century presents theology with the need to think of its own end, these are questions of primary importance.

None of this may, to be sure, have any direct bearing upon the theme of theology at the end of the twentieth century. But one of the things that become clear through this discussion is that the theologies represented by Taylor, Altizer, and Winquist reflect the openness of the present situation. They are cultural theologies rather than church theologies or philosophies of religion, and they reflect the fact that some of the sources currently most provocative of theological thought are neither ecclesiastical nor overtly religious. From this it is not difficult to draw the conclusion that one of the questions facing theology at the end of the century is that of the extent to which such currents can be formed into a theology.

The Self

The question of the self appears more in Winquist's and in Taylor's discussions than in Altizer's. Here I shall restrict myself to Winquist's account.

Winquist asserts that understanding the possibilities for theology at the end and turn of the century requires giving an account of the "subversion of Enlightenment and modernist understandings of the self" that was brought about by the critiques coming from Marx, Nietzsche, and Freud. Essentially these critiques attack the belief that the self is fully transparent to itself; they attack the idea that I can always know, for example, what the motives of my actions or the contents of my thoughts are. The three critiques do not have a common basis. In Marx, the basis is the notion that what the self recognizes or puts forth as truth is dependent upon a class interest. In Nietzsche, it is the related, but more general notion that ideas are expressions of the will to power, which in the end is, as Heidegger put it, the nihilistic will to will. In Freud, the basis is the concept of an unconscious mechanism that underlies conscious mental activity. (Whether the Freudian unconscious really has the character of a mechanism can be left here as a dispute among Freud interpreters.) Instead of refuting or dispelling these critiques, Winquist takes up the task of thinking in the tradition that has arisen from them. They are not, as they once were, the bêtes noires of theology but the pathbreakers toward a theology that is no longer ontotheological in character. "Ontotheology" here refers to a certain way in which the concepts of being and God are understood and related both to each other and to other concepts. In the current discussion, the rejection of ontotheology (a term apparently coined by Kant) has its roots in Heidegger's essay "The Onto-theo-logical Constitution [*Verfassung*] of Metaphysics." In that essay, Heidegger asked how God got into philosophy. He answered that God got into philosophy because the difference between being and beings remained unthought, and he suggested that the atheism of contemporary philosophy might be closer to the "godly God" than was the supreme being of ontotheology. The rejections of ontotheology, however, owe as much to Derrida and the French Heideggerian literature. What is being rejected is the possibility of finding a first, an irreducible principle, upon which everything is based and from which everything can be derived. A clear example of ontotheology in this sense of the word is a doctrine of God in which God is understood as the first, uncaused (or self-caused) cause of all things and the supreme being from which all other beings are derived. By contrast, such theologies as those of Schleiermacher and Tillich do not fit well under this characterization of ontotheology; and, in fact, Heidegger's own account of theology in his essay *Phänomenologie und Theologie* of 1928 is not unlike the account given by Schleiermacher at the beginning of his dogmatics, *The Christian Faith*. Even Schleiermacher's use of "the whence," rather than "the cause," to designate the intentionality in religious feeling—the whence of the feeling of absolute dependence—indicates a break with this kind of ontotheology. Tillich's theology does correlate being and God, and does adopt the affirmation "God is being itself," but not in the manner of what either Heidegger or the French Heideggerians call ontology. In any case, however, it is the tradition of the three "masters of suspicion" (as Ricoeur called them) that Winquist wants to use as the setting for a kind of theological thinking that is not ontotheological.

The guideline is provided by the way in which key metonyms can orient or give a certain turn to a whole discourse, to a whole way of talking and writing about a subject. "Metonym" refers broadly to any word used in a nonliteral sense in order to "defamiliarize" the ordinary. Speaking of ultimate reality by using the metonym "God" is given as one example: the metonym "tropes" the discourse, it gives the whole discourse a certain turn even while it leaves intact the meanings of the other words in the discourse. Am I right in concluding that Winquist here rejects Ricoeur's metaphorical approach in favor of this metonymical one? Metaphor is, Ricoeur says in opposition to Aristotle, a feature not of individual words but of language-units that are at least sentences. Metaphors are new meanings created out of the contradiction in meaning between the sense of the individual words and the sense of the larger unit.

That metonyms affect a whole discourse by the turn they give it is the context for Winquist's discussion of the importance for theology of Lacan's orders of the imaginary, the symbolic, and the real in the self's perception of itself. The first self-perception, as in infants, is nothing more than a fragmentary perception of the body. But a mirror image introduces the order of the imaginary: a mirror reflection presents an external view of the whole body. The move from the imaginary to the symbolic order occurs by way of discourse, that is, by an understanding of the mirror image *as* imaginary instead of as an empirical reality, to which one might flee for refuge from the fragmentation of perception (as though I could see in a mirror the totality of my body that I otherwise perceive only fragmentarily). The imaginary is more than a repetition of the original perception when it is understood as imaginary and put into discourse; for an image put into discourse belongs to the order of the symbolic.

These steps, if I have understood him rightly, are what Winquist appropriates from Lacan. But another consideration is equally important: there is a "bar" between the symbolic and the real. We have no way of passing from a symbolic representation to an apprehension of the real as such. The real always remains the other-than-itself to which the symbolic order points but which it does not imitate or make present; the real is a "heterological" element in the symbolic. That relation, in which what is intended by the symbolic (the reality of the "it") is meant by but absent from the symbol, is a relation of "desire" rather than of "description." Symbols, therefore, represent a desire of the real; they do not provide a description of the real; they have in them the fusion of absence and presence that characterizes desire. Against the background of these orders of the imaginary and the symbolic, the "dismantling of the subject," which appears in contemporary human sciences, amounts to the recognition that we have no intuition, no direct perception, of the I who is the subject of the texts we read. What we have, rather, is a text itself. Our interpretation of the text constructs a subjectivity in the text. Am I right in assuming that these assertions are a variation on Derrida's theme that there is no transcendental signified, that is to say, that we have no intuition or cognition of a reality or of a subject that is not in some way already mediated by language?[2]

To this point I think I follow the line of thought drawn by Winquist. But after this point, several things are not clear to me. I shall try to indicate what these unclarities are by posing several questions.

In the discussion of the unity of apperception, there seems to be a shifting between the subject who is the reader and the subject who is the author of a text or, more generally, between the subject who is I and other subjects. The "unity of apperception," if one thinks of what Kant meant by that term, is the unity of the perceiving subject—we apperceive the ego as the subjective origin of our perceptions along with our perceptions of empirical objects and our pure perceptions of time and space. The post-Kantian controversy about an intellectual intuition had to do with whether there can even be such an intuition of the ego. That question, however, is different from the question whether I can intuit, or otherwise perceive, *another* subject through the statements of a text produced by that subject. For the ego that is my own is always the point of view from which I see or interpret or apprehend. It is the zero-point of all my actions (Blanchot's "terrifyingly ancient" and Levinas's "unrepresentable before" to which Taylor refers?), whereas the ego of some other person, who is the author of a text or the maker of statements, is within the world upon which I gaze. The I that I am as this-one-here is different from the I of any other one who appears in a body or a text to this "me." These two aspects of the question of the subject are treated in the paragraphs mentioned as though they were one and the same: "We cannot assume a silent unity behind the statements. . . . We can construct diagrams . . . and then reference these constructs as a subjectivity in the text. . . . the subject experiences as it is experienced in its constructedness." In the first two sentences the subject seems to be the author of any text that I may be reading. In the third sentence the subject seems to be I who am reading the text, not the subject who is the author of the text. Is the distinction between these two subjects not essential? Is it erased here?

True, who "I" am appears in how I read the text of another, and not only in the text I write myself. Even so, if the one who wrote the text I am reading is not myself, then the text as I read it contains the other's "who" as well as mine. Is the mixing of these two subjects done by design here? If so, I wonder about the justification for doing so.

When we consider (1) the relation of a representation to the thing represented (or of the signifier to the signified), (2) the relation between the subjectivity in the text before us and the author who is behind the text, and (3) the relation between the subjectivity deposited in our discourse and our own self as the zero-point of that discourse, we are in a sense dealing with three aspects of one and the same problem. Who I myself am emerges out of the interplay between my I as such (which I never see) and the subjectivity that appears as the shaper of my discourse. Similarly, who the real author of a text is emerges out of the interplay between the subjectivity that appears in the shaping of the text and the author in himself. And, also similarly, what a real thing is appears only in the interplay between the signifiers and the signified. But this similarity among the three relations is limited (if not partly deceptive) because I have an access to my own interiority (even when the contents of that interiority are not fully transparent to me) which I do not have to the interiority of someone else or to the noumenal side of an object that I perceive. For this reason there is an irreducible difference between the subjective being indicated in the statement "I am this-one-here-now" and the subjective being indicated in the statement "You are (he, she is) that-one-there-now."

That difference seems to be incontestable. It seems to be ineradicable too, even if we grant that I who read someone else's writing am in a way rewriting it as well. Does it also play a role in connection with the notion of the unconscious which, along with the real, is Winquist's theme? One answer might be to say that "the unconscious" lies deeper than any self-awareness and designates a dimension at which the difference between the subject who "I" am and the subject who another person is no longer matters. For in such a case, the mechanism of the unconscious in myself is no more apparent to me in my interior self-awareness than it is apparent to me in my awareness of personal subjects other than myself; I have access to it only by some such method as psychoanalytical interpretation. But will such an answer be tenable if, along with Lacan but contrary to mechanistic inter-

pretations of Freud, the unconscious is held to be not a mechanism but a subjectivity?[3] At this point I am raising the question
only for further clarification, not to argue a position.

Decentering of the Self

In the critique of ontotheology or the ontotheological tradition,
both Taylor and Winquist make references to the decentering or
dispersal of the self and set this recognition in opposition to a
Kantian transcendental ego or to Tillich's notion of a fully centered self. But I wonder whether more has been made of the phenomenon of self-dispersal than can be justified. This wonder leads
me to formulate a number of questions.

The self-world polarity in Tillich's ontological analysis is closer
to Heidegger's kind of phenomenology than it is to a Kantian transcendental analysis. The ideas of self and world, or subject and object, are derived by analyzing the structure that is contained in
the asking of the most basic question one can think of asking,
"Why is there anything at all?" The existence of such a question
implies, at a minimum, an asker and an asked-about. Tillich designates these two elements epistemologically as "subject" and
"object" and ontologically as "self" and "world." The test of
whether an element is ontological, that is, necessarily implied as
part of the structure of a phenomenon (in this case the phenomenon is the ontological question), is similar to the test applied to
determine logical necessity. The universality of a logical principle, such as the principle of identity, is tested by whether even a
denial of the principle formally implies the principle. As Fichte's
Wissenschaftslehre first demonstrated, the principles of identity
and difference are by this test equally original and universal. Similarly, the universality of an ontological proposition is tested by
whether an actual denial of it must make use of it. Thus, if I were
to contend that the ontological question, not in its formal structure but as a question actually asked, does not imply a subject and
an object, the test is whether I can actually make such a denial
without implying the subject-object structure. Does my denial
imply a structure having the elements of *someone* making the denial and *something* being denied? This sort of ontological concept
of self (subject) and world (object) does not immediately say anything about how many people are interested in ontological analysis, just as the rules of formal logic do not say anything about how
many people have actually studied logic or would even be inter-

ested in doing so. Nor does it say anything about what kind of world we can know, or how we know it, or what kind of self the self of self-awareness and self-interpretation might be. It says only that the ontological structure is inescapable. Hence, the critique of ontotheology does not seem to me to say anything about *this* kind of ontology at all, and I wonder whether the application can be made to Tillich in quite so direct a fashion as Winquist makes it, though I do agree that Tillich's theology of absolute paradox, stated as early as 1913, may amount to the same conclusion as Winquist's.

Beyond this, both Taylor's and Winquist's accounts of subjectivity seem to overlook the distinction between two concepts of a transcendental subject. Do they really do so? Let me elaborate the question. On the one hand, it is easy to grant, for the sake of argument at least, that there is no transcendental subjectivity in the sense of a set of norms or criteria, or a structure of subjectivity, that everyone everywhere would recognize as valid. What counts as moral or as reasonable may very well differ from culture to culture and from one historical period to another. Hence, Kant's contention that there is only one idea (the idea of God) which can make moral experience intelligible (and not leave one caught in the contradiction between the unlimitedness of the moral demand and the limitations of actual deeds, or in the contradiction between reason and nature) and his contention that therefore everyone postulates the idea of God as a necessity of reason may not be tenable. Such contentions may not be irrefutable in the way that laws of logic are formally irrefutable. One may grant this for the sake of argument, even though there do seem to be some universals—every language, for example, seems to contain a form corresponding to what we know as a subject-predicate proposition (saying something about something), and there does seem to be something on the order of an identifiable ontological structure, in Tillich's sense of that phrase. Even if this is granted, however, it does not follow that there is any way in which one can escape from being rooted in a singular, unexchangeable here-now that is indicated by the word *I*. Both Taylor and Winquist seem to suggest that such an escape can be made. The suggestion is less clear in Taylor, for he does cite Blanchot's reference to the "unthinkable ancestor" despite seeming to adopt Altizer's notion of the anonymity of the self.

Can an escape from the I-ness of the I be made? Even if the full content of subjectivity, including one's own subjectivity, is a di-

versity that is dispersed through many texts, so that who I am as a
subject is revealed to me as well as to others by the way in which I
talk and write, this does not cancel the unity indicated by a root-
edness in the I as such. At least, I do not see how it does so; and I
seek further illumination from Taylor and Winquist on this point.

What Is Theology

What is theology? Today it is frequently defined as a reflection on
faith or a reflective interpretation of what is present prereflec-
tively in the act of faith. In theological schoolbooks of an older
time the question was posed with a double possibility in mind.
Theology could be the discourse (*logos*) about God or things divine (θεός) or the θεῖον. Or it could be the talk about God by God,
God's own talk of God, *sermo de Deo a Deo seipso*. If that question is put to the three contributors to this volume, the answers
seem to be somewhat different among themselves.

The answer in Altizer's essay seems to be clear. Theology is, as
the word indicates, talk about God. More exactly, it is a historical
narrative told as a narrative of what God has done. It begins with
God's revelation of the divine name I Am, and it ends when the
speaking of that name is silent, that is, when no one hears any
transcendent voice saying "I am." Altizer's is a kind of biblical
theology, but with a considerably expanded canon. The events in
the narrative are not only the usual ones from Exodus to Resurrection; they also include such events of "secular" history as the
French Revolution and such nonbiblical authors as Augustine,
Dante, Milton, Blake, Nietzsche, and Joyce. Furthermore, the
superscription of all these events, or the one event that is unfolding in all of them, is the event entitled the death of God. That
event is the beginning and end of history. History begins with the
self-naming of God and ends with the silencing of that name.
That is to say, it ends when the I Am, which at first was the special name of God, is the naming of the self of anyone and everyone
(Joyce's "Here Comes Everybody"). What is the relation of this
theological history to "real" history? That question, I must admit, is one to which I do not see a clear answer. That admission
can here provide Altizer with an occasion to clear things up. Even
if the history included in this theology were quite individualis-
tically conceived, however, so that no one else would recognize
the events included in it as having quite the significance ascribed
to them, this would still be an intelligible concept of theology. It

would amount to a reading of all that happens from the point of view of the question What is God doing? What God *is* (eternally) doing is, in Altizer's theology, giving up deity. "Real" history is the scene in which this deed is actualized more and more widely and deeply.

Winquist, I think, gives a different answer to the question "What is theology?" Theology is the language game (if "language game" is the equivalent of "discursive practice") in which one speaks of anything or everything in such a way as to "defamiliarize" it. It is talking and writing in such a way that the otherwise familiar becomes unfamiliar. That is one side of the matter. The other side is that, when directed toward texts that are themselves traditionally theological, theology is a reading that reads against the grain of theological language, against its totalizing. Theology is inherently totalizing. But the totalizing has to be undone; that is what, in part, the "subversion of modern understandings of the self" amounts to. What seems to me valuable in this suggestion is that it does not overlook the totalizing tendency in theology as such but rather reckons with the question of how that tendency can be both acknowledged and relativized by the way the theological language is read.

But how does this work out? When "God" is inserted into discourse, the "play of signifiers shifts its meaning with the metonymic troping of the discourse without changing any of the other words." Let us suppose that the "play of signifiers" refers to the way in which the words of a text refer back and forth to each other within a whole context as well as to something beyond the text. For example, when we read or hear "Four score and seven years ago" from Lincoln's *Gettysburg Address*, we also think of such other words as "our fathers," "this continent," "a new nation," in the same address and in other texts recalling them; and today, after feminist criticisms of language, the words "our fathers" have even other cross-referencing. That is the play of the signifiers, the way in which the words of a text refer back and forth to each other and not only to something outside the text. When "God" is inserted into the discourse, the "meaning" of this play of signifiers is shifted. What would that mean in this illustration? What is the "meaning" of that play in the example cited? Let us say that the meaning of the play of signifiers (not the play itself) is the sense of the critical nature of the time at which these words were spoken. In hearing these words, we also apprehend that meaning. How is the meaning shifted, if we insert the word *God* into the text? Suppose that we say, "Four score and seven years ago *God created* on this continent a new nation." Have we merely ruined Lincoln's text? How is the meaning shifted by the insertion of the "un-assimilable trope" of "God created"? There is still a play of signifiers in the text, the back and forth referring that goes on among the different words: "new nation," "four score," "seven," and so on. But now there is a new meaning to that play. What is this new meaning?

We have added a trope that cannot be assimilated because "God created" cannot be reduced to a concept, as though "God created" ruled out "our fathers brought forth." How does that addition change the meaning of the cross-referencing among the words and with reality? Certain "figurations will dominate a discourse [after first principles have been given up] by pressuring the differential play of textual and intertextual referencing in the complex of knowledge and power." How does the addition of "God creates" (or a similar trope) "pressure" the "differential play" of the signifiers in it?

An additional feature of Winquist's account of theology is its reference to reflexivity. There is no epistemology outside theology that can be used to gauge theology. We cannot get rid of the theological character of the assessment of theology. "We cannot turn to theology without fully implicating our inquiry in the heterological infrastructures of nomad subjectivities and at the same time the textual surfaces of the ontotheological tradition." What is a heterological infrastructure? An infrastructure is a structure "below" some other structure. The organized way in which times and rooms get assigned for teaching courses at an educational institution is, for example, an infrastructure for the structure of education. Mechanisms for administering government programs are an infrastructure of the structure of government. In Tillich's ontological analysis, the self-world relation is an infrastructure of the structure of being in the world. If one speaks of the heterological infrastructure of subjectivities, what is the *structure* in relation to which the infrastructure of subjectivities is *infra?* Is it the ontological structure? And is this infrastructure an infrastructure in the way that an administrative mechanism is an infrastructure to governing or in the way that a self-world relation is the infrastructure of the grammatical or logical structure of asking a question or in the way that English grammar is the infrastructure of spoken and written English? Is every infrastructure heterological rather than ontological—is it a structure of the *other* of being rather than of *being?* As an in-fra*structure* is the structure of multiple subjectivities something found in all subjectivities? Or does calling it a heterological in-frastructure mean that it is a structure which makes every subjec-tivity different from other subjectivities, hence, a structuring of the difference among them? These are some of the questions indicating my unclarity about the way subjectivity bears upon theology.

Taylor's answer to the question "What is theology?" is impor-tant for understanding how, or what kind of, theology has come to an end at the end of the twentieth century. If the God whose death Nietzsche declared is the moralistic God, then a certain kind of theology, namely, a theology of accusation and punishment, is no longer possible wherever people no longer believe such a God to be a real power. One might then, along with Ricoeur, look for a theology in which freedom and the love for creation (a higher form of consolation) have replaced fear of punishment and the de-sire for protection.[4] Similarly, if it is the metaphysical God, the God identical with a supreme being, whose death is declared, one might follow Heidegger and look for a theology of the God more godly than the God of ontotheological metaphysics. Taylor's con-ception of an a/theology seems to be something different from ei-ther of these two suggestions. But in what way? Indications are given in his reference to "the nothing that [metaphysical? every?] theology leaves unthought" and in the mention of a dialogue with an other that cannot be named (Beckett) over against a mono-logue of the Absolute with itself (Hegel). And some questions are elicited by the notion of writing "the impossibility of theology by writing an a/theology in which God is always missing" for which "it is necessary to rethink the death of God by thinking the way one dies." The questions: If the way one dies is never as an "I do" but always as an "I can," then is the impossibility of theology a mirror image of the possibility of my-death? So that "end" is what I *always can* but *never do* do (in that sense, the end is always in the coming but never gets here for me) and speak-as-God (theol-ogy) is what I *never can* but *always do* do? If so, have we, after all, converged upon the point at which the silence of a transcendent "I am" (as in Altizer) is the speaking-of-God that I always do do along with what is said in what I say as my self on my own?

In any case, it is painting to which Taylor first turns in order to indicate what the end of the twentieth century may mean for the-ology. One aspect of it has to do with Yves Klein's blue; and another has to do with his erasure of the frame. The blue is a representation of Lost Eden; the erasure is an incarnation of the sacred in the profane. Klein's blue monochromes "dissolve forms into an undifferentiated unity of color that actualizes the primordial identity of subject and object"; the blue is not "the mere absence or negation of being" but "embodies the plenitude of being's presence." Nowhere in modern art "does the erasure of the frame reach such proportions," for it "realizes the full incarnation of the sacred in the profane." The further analysis of Yves Klein's blue provides an indication of what is meant by the nothing and how it is connected with theology or a/theology: the end that is to be thought at the end of theology "becomes actual" in the "full presence embodied in modern art." By contrast with Klein, the nothing in Fontana's *Tagli* is not the no thing that *is* in all things but implies, rather, "a lack of being that neither exists nor does not exist"; Fontana reinscribes "the margin of difference" that Klein, "like all modernists, struggles to erase or efface." Klein's paintings are "painterly versions of classical negative theology." Taylor concludes: "The end for which both theologian and painter strive is unitive ecstasy with the all." "The return to Eden is the apocalyptic union of Alpha and Omega."

Let me pose a few general questions which come to mind in connection with the suggestions made in these quotations and related passages in the essay. First, does the end of theology (at the end of this century) mean the absorption of what was theology into a different kind of "thinking" (much in the way that Heidegger proposed what there was to think at the end of metaphysics)? Put differently, the question might be this: Does the end of metaphysical theology (the theology of God as the supreme being) mean the absorption of theology into a kind of thinking for which the word or concept of God no longer plays a role? Is "the all" a replacement of "God"? If it is, does this cancel the difference between the concepts of universe and of God? Does a thinking of the all bear a resemblance to the panentheism of Schelling or of Hartshorne? Second, if the "plenitude of being's presence" (in Klein's blue) is the same as the restoration of Lost Eden, are God and being identical? Third, is it Fontana or is it Klein who comes closer to showing what theology at the end (of the century or of itself) has to think about? Or do they represent two sides of the same matter— the "not" that is in everything and the "not" that neither is nor is not in anything? Finally, we can distinguish "nothing" as meaning the "not" of not-this, not-that, and not-anything (the nothing of one form of negative theology) from the negative expressed in "not anything and not nothing either." If we combine the nothingness of Fontana and the nothingness of Klein, do we have the equivalent of a nothingness that is not anything but not nothing either? And is *this* concept, in turn, the equivalent of a nonmetaphysical ("nonontotheological") concept of God and the subject of an other theology?

NOTES

1. It may not distinguish between the "I" and the "you," since it is also true that a "You can die" cannot be changed into a "You did die" either. Even so, we can say something like that to a deceased person whereas we cannot say it to ourselves. So the connection of this pure possibility with the "I" is clearer than with the "you."

2. That there is no transcendental signified does not mean, as some of Derrida's critics have understood it, that there is nothing outside the text. But it does mean we have no experience or knowledge of the referent without the use of *some* language. If someone asks me what the word *tree* refers to and I reply by pointing to an object with my finger, it may seem that we have a case of seeing the referent apart from the word referring to it. But my gesture of pointing to the tree could not point out the object meant if the gesture were not understood, that is to say, if it were not a language, even though nonverbal. If the gesture were not understood as a signifier, the person to whom I was trying to point out an object would not know whether it was my finger or something else that the word *tree* has as its referent. It is in that sense that there is no transcendental signified, no pure object unmediated by any signifiers whatsoever and having no signifying quality in turn.

3. See Lacan's comments on Freud's "Wo Es war, soll Ich werden" in Jacques Lacan, *Ecrits: A Selection*, trans. Alan Sheridan (New York: Norton, 1977), pp. 128 f.

4. Paul Ricoeur, *The Conflict of Interpretations* (Evanston: Northwestern Univ. Press, 1974), pp. 460, 467.

6

REPLIES:

THE SELF-REALIZATION

OF DEATH

WHAT IS most missing from Robert P. Scharlemann's response to "The Beginning and Ending of Revelation" is both the historical and the apocalyptic, and in this context the historical *is* the apocalyptic, for it is finally that apocalypse which is revelation itself. At no point is the absence of the historical more manifest than in Scharlemann's inability to respond to the French Revolution as the first universal historical event, not being able to understand how as such it is profoundly different from the advent of Greek philosophy or Frederick II, and is so not simply because it transformed consciousness, but rather because it transformed historical actuality itself, a transformation that was historically destined to be universally embodied throughout the world. This is that historical event which fundamentally ended the premodern world, just as is it that historical event which fully and finally actualized the death of God, so that to refuse the French Revolution as a universal historical event is to refuse the historical actualization of the death of God. So likewise to identify apocalypse as the unveiling of the hidden God is to refuse apocalypse as the total transformation of all and everything, and most particularly so a total transformation of what both revelation and faith have named as God. Total presence is not the total presence of the transcendent God, as in Psalm 139, but rather the total presence of apocalypse, an apocalypse that Jesus proclaimed and parabolically enacted as the immediate advent of the Kingdom of God.

And Kingdom of God is not the reign of God, or not in the New

Testament as opposed to the Old, for it is that New Jerusalem in which God will be "all in all," and therefore will not be and cannot be "God." Nor is it arbitrary to understand Christianity as an apocalyptic faith, or to understand the French Revolution as the final advent of a new universal humanity, for such understanding is simply the product of the modern historical consciousness itself. In this perspective, the French Revolution was an apocalyptic event, even as the English Revolution was both potentially and actually so before it, and therefore our modern revolutionary history is an apocalyptic history, and thus a history in continuity with biblical history, or in continuity with that biblical history and consciousness which itself was eschatological or apocalyptic. Now nothing is more important in that history than the historical advent of self-consciousness, a self-consciousness that apparently did not actually or fully exist until the advent of Christianity, and a self-consciousness that clearly was an apocalyptic consciousness, which is to say a consciousness profoundly grounded in its own death or end, a death whose ground was established by the death of I AM. That is the death which is I AM's alone, but it is also that death which establishes and realizes the "I alone," an I which never previously had been manifest to itself as such, and an I which can be so manifest to itself only by the actualization of its own end or death. Paul's letters are, of course, the first written embodiment of this self-actualization of death, but this self-actualization of death was at the center of the Augustinian revolution, a revolution that gave us the categories of the personal I and the individual and interior will, and these categories existed at the center of our Western history until the ending of that history in our own world.

Now to understand the death of I AM as the origin of our history, and the origin of our self-consciousness as well, is to understand our history as both a total and an actual history, a history that really occurred, and a history that is all consuming. Moreover, this is also a progressive and a sequential history, it evolves only gradually in time, and it occurs in multiple and integrally structured events. So, too, this is a history that has its beginning in the self-naming or self-revelation of I AM, and its ending in the self-silencing or self-annihilation of I AM. Both of these events are in some sense embodiments or actualizations of the death of God, but they are not simply identical events, as witness the overwhelming historical transformations which occurred between them. It is the archaic myth of eternal return which dissolves historical actuality, and even if that myth was reborn in late modernity, it was reborn in historical actuality itself, an actuality which is the embodiment of the self-annihilation of God. This is the nothingness that is now our actual nothingness, and it is a new nothingness, a nothingness that is historically new, for even if it has a ground in an Augustinian nothingness, it is now a total nothingness, and a total nothingness that is a total abyss. If this is a nothingness that not even a Heidegger could fully name, it is a nothingness that dominates the late modern or postmodern imagination, just as it is a nothingness that all of us know and realize in a new and fully anonymous society and consciousness.

Scharlemann asks, if death is the *possibility* most my own (and a possibility never convertible to an actuality), is this same phenomenon of death the *actuality* most God's own (and an actuality with never an antecedent possibility)? Clearly, from his point of view, the answer to this question is yes. But to answer this question affirmatively is to accept the question as such, and that is to affirm that the death which is my ownmost possiblity is identical with the death that is God's ownmost actuality. I would rather affirm that the death which is my ownmost possibility is a consequence of the death which is God's ownmost actuality, that the actuality of that death is inseparable from God's identity as God, as the fully revealing and therefore finally incarnate God, and that the actuality of that death is finally apocalypse itself, so that the death and the nothingness which is most and now newly our own is the hither side for us of that Kingdom of God which is the death of I AM. This would entail an understanding of Kingdom of God as the full and final actualization of the self-annihilation of I AM, a self-annihilation which is all that we can know of the grace of resurrection, and a grace which we know when we know our death as being fully and finally our own. But it is our own only because it is God's own, the death which is our ownmost possibility exists nowhere but within the horizon of the death of I AM, a death which is itself both the source and the ground of the self-realization of death, a self-realization which is simultaneously both our historical origin and our apocalyptic destiny.

It is only in my ownmost death, my full and actual death, that there is no distinction between my "I am" and the I AM of God. And that death is certainly not something that I always *can* do but never *do* do! It is far rather something that has been given me, and wholly given me, and something that has been done or has occurred in that history which is both our origin and our destiny. For there is no I which is simply and only an I—this is an abstraction with no actual or real existence—and hence it is no actual possibility for anyone. So likewise the speculative thinking of Hegel is not the thinking of the autonomous ego or of the I as such; it is a thinking that is possible only within a single moment of history, and only as a consequence of both that thinking and that history which preceded it. The "speculative Good Friday" is the speculative Good Friday, and not a speculation which would have been possible or actual outside of the Christian horizon of consciousness. Nor would Heidegger's understanding of death have been possible outside of that horizon, for such an understanding of death is wholly alien to Greek philosophy and the classical world, just as it is alien to Buddhism and the Eastern world. Only in the Golgotha of absolute Spirit is death a final and ultimate event, and that is an event which has actually occurred, and occurred so as to establish and to ground what we have known both as history and as self-consciousness.

Both that history and that self-consciousness are now ending, and ending in our historical actuality, an actuality that we can neither flee nor evade, and an actuality ending everything that we once knew as hope and as faith. Night has fallen upon our history, and upon the center of our self-consciousness as well, a night which is a new and total nothingness, but a nothingness which we are finally called to know as grace. That is a call which is a mystery to us, a call to speak our darkness, and to speak it so as to realize it as our own. For we know that our darkness is our own, it did not simply fall upon us, for it evolved out of a history going back to our very beginning, a beginning which is present once again if only as the beginning of our end. Ending is everywhere about us, and it is the ending of our beginning, a beginning that we can know to be our unique beginning, and know it as perhaps we have never known it before. For now we can know the very advent of revelation, the advent of a unique and absolute beginning, the beginning of a speech which is speech and speech alone, and therefore the ending of a silence which is all in all. That beginning is our origin, an origin that is marked by call, a call ending an original silence, and thus a call disrupting and reversing an original quiescence. Now such a quiescence appears to be upon our horizon once again, but it is not truly upon our horizon if we know it as a dark and negative emptiness, an abysmal chaos that can never either pass into a total calm and peace or undergo a repetition into a truly new beginning.

The very presence of call to us can only be the call of grace, a grace that is present even in that abyss which we know to be our own, for that abyss refuses and negates every nostalgia for an earlier or even a primordial moment of time. True calm is precisely what is impossible for us, and impossible because of the very presence of our abyss, an abyss denying us even the peace of death, for there is no death upon our horizon which cannot truly be our own. And death is our own because we can know it as our ultimate origin, an origin that mythically can be named as our expulsion from paradise, and theologically can be named as Crucifixion, a crucifixion that is the origin of an actually negative and doubled consciousness, a consciousness that is alienated from itself, and precisely in that self-alienation is conscious of itself. While the self-consciousness inaugurated by that self-alienation is now ending about and within us, it has not simply been forgotten or ended, as witness the fact that innocence is impossible for us, and impossible if only because we cannot evade the presence of death. For we cannot evade or escape a death that is truly our own, a death that is truly our destiny, and is our destiny because of who we are, a destiny apart from which we would simply and only be empty, as opposed to that dark and abysmal emptiness that we know ourselves to be.

If *Oedipus at Colonus* is the highest moment of Greek tragedy, a tragedy realizing a death that is inaudible and invisible in its very nature, and thereby and only thereby a death that here can be accepted and affirmed, the Crucifixion is a death that is fully actual and manifest, and a death whose very actuality is finally and irrevocably affirmed. Nor does that death stand isolated and alone; it is the culmination of what the Christian knows as revelation, and it inaugurates an interior movement toward death that we know to be our innermost identity, and an identity that can only culminate in a final and ultimate apocalypse. If it was Paul who first knew the inseparability of crucifixion and apocalypse, an inseparability that has again and again been enacted in our history, in our own time an apocalypse of death has become universal and total, and final and irrevocable as well. So it is that our abyss is a new nothingness, but it nevertheless remains a nothingness of death, and precisely as such now calls upon us for acceptance and affirmation, for it is a death that we inescapably know to be our own. And we know it to be our own for our origin lies in ultimate death, the death of Crucifixion, and therefore a death that is an absolute actualization and realization of death, for it is a death that is finally apocalypse itself. If our history has ever been a movement toward that apocalypse, the seeds of apocalypse have also been sown within us, and sown by that sower who is the Crucified God.

UNENDING STROKES

Patch-work—Patchwork

Self-commentary? What a bore! I had no other solution than to *re-write* myself—at a distance, a great distance—here and now: to add to the books, to the themes, to the memories, to the texts, another utterance, without ever knowing whether it is about my past or my present that I am speaking. Whereby I cast over the written work, over the past body and the past corpus, barely brushing against it, a kind of patchwork, a rhapsodic quilt consisting of stitched squares. Far from reaching the core of the matter, I remain on the surface . . . ; reaching the core, depth, profundity, belongs to others.[1]

I HAVE nothing left to say. Always nothing left to say. But how to say it? To say it again? And again, and again? When Duchamp had nothing left to paint, he stopped painting and started playing chess. But this gesture is too literal or too symbolic—I am not sure which. To paint nothing by not painting is a reversal that undoes nothing. To undo this undoing might be to do nothing. Perhaps this is all that is left when (the) all has left. There is no core of the mat(t)er to reach . . . only surfaces. Surfaces that are not always superficial.

* * * * *

Why has Scharlemann "ended" his "Response" with asterisks (not one, but five) instead of a period? Are these stars ill-fated and thus his "end" disastrous rather than apocalyptic? What *is* an asterisk?

> *Asterisk:* Late Latin *asteriscus,* from Greek *asteriskos,* little star, asterisk, from *aster,* star. 1. A little star. 2. Anything shaped or radiating like a star; in the *Eastern Church* a star-shaped instrument of gold or silver placed above the chalice and paten to prevent the veil from touching the elements. 3. The figure of a star used in writing and printing as a reference to a note at the foot or margin of

the page, to indicate the omission of words or letters, to distinguish words and phrases as conjectural, obscure, or bearing some other specified character, as a dividing mark, or for similar typographical purposes.

Scharlemann's asterisks reference nothing; there is nothing at the margin of the page. Do they, then, mark the site of an omission of words or letters? What words? Which letters? What is Scharlemann not telling us? Or are the asterisks dividing marks? How do marks divide? What do marks divide? The asterisks might have nothing to do with writing. Perhaps they suspend the (invisible) veil that must not touch the elements. But why must the eucharistic elements be veiled? If the elements remain veiled can apocalypse ever take place? Is disaster anything other than the impossibility of apocalypse?

Disaster: dis + astro, star, from Latin *astrum,* from Greek *astron.*

I will linger with several of the questions that Scharlemann poses.

* * * * *

. . . I cast over the written work, over the past body and the past corpus . . .

One day there is life. A man, for example, in the best of health, not even old, with no history of illness. Everything is as it was, as it will always be. He goes from one day to the next, minding his own business, dreaming only of the life that lies before him. And then, suddenly, it happens there is death. A man lets out a little sigh, he slumps down in his chair, and it is death. The suddenness of it leaves no room for thought, gives the mind no chance to seek out a word that might comfort it. We are left with nothing but death, the irreducible fact of our own mortality. Death after a long illness we can accept with resignation. Even accidental death we can ascribe to fate. But for a man to die of no apparent cause, for a man to die simply because he is a man, brings us so close to the invisible boundary between life and death that we no longer know which side we are on. Life becomes death, and it is as if this death has owned this life all along. Death without warning. Which is to say: life stops.[2]

"What is the End?"

I cannot, of course, answer this question. I can, however, suggest why it is unanswerable. The very propriety of the question renders it improper. The question "What *is* . . . ?" remains within the economy of being and nonbeing. As such, it follows the logic of ontotheology according to which being and nonbeing are binary or dialectical opposites. To define the isness of something is to establish its identity and secure its difference from everything else. If, however, the end is interpreted in terms of the disaster, it eludes the logic of ontotheology. The disastrous end neither is nor is not. Always drawing near without ever arriving, the end is never present and yet is not simply absent. Since the end never appears, it is not a phenomenon *sensu strictissimo* and hence cannot be subjected to phenomenological analysis. The end that is not the end *of* theology marks the end of phenomenology. A/theological thinking is not, as Scharlemann suggests, based upon "intrinsic and phenomenological grounds." To the contrary, a/theology solicits nonphenomena that remain exterior to every logos. I have tried to think the unthinkable end by reading death through disaster and disaster through death.

> *"What is the nature of the combination*
>
> *of the fulfillment [of the self]*
>
> *and the possibility [of death]?"*

Death inevitably is by stroke. *Un coup* . . . It is always sudden, *tout à coup* . . . even when it comes slowly. One moment there is life. And then . . . More I cannot say. The suddenness of it leaves no room for thought . . .

I do not approach death, even as I age. *Death* approaches . . . always approaches from elsewhere. Elsewhere is not beyond but is near . . . proximate . . . close. Close but never present, death does not appear, or it "appears" as withdrawing. In this approaching withdrawal, death closes. This closure opens an incurable wound.

The nonabsent absence of death is not, as Scharlemann claims, "the authentic phenomenon par excellence, the phenomenon that most distinguishes the self in its propriety, its own I-ness or *Eigentlichkeit*." Authenticity, Heidegger argues, presupposes that *I* face death—*my own* death. But I cannot *face* death and death is never my own. Death averts, turns away. Never seen face-to-face, death is glimpsed, if at all, only in a play of masks. The masks of death disperse rather than consolidate the I. More precisely, the proximity of death exposes the I itself as a death mask.

Scharlemann disagrees:

What Taylor suggests about the futurity (the adventivity, or *Zu-künftigkeit*) of the existential end (my-death) is clearly true. The end is by its very nature always in the coming but never getting here (for "me"). But I wonder whether this is really an objection to the connection between death and the propriety of the self as I. Does it really undermine the contention, familiar to us since Heidegger's analysis in *Being and Time,* that death is the possibility most my *own?* It does not seem to me to do so unless one overlooks the difference between possibility and actuality.

While Scharlemann freely admits that death is never actual *for me,* he insists that death is "sheer possibility" for me. "Sheer" or "pure" possibility is possibility that can never become actuality. As such, sheer possibility is what "I, as subject in the first person singular, always (only) *can* do but never *do* do." So understood, possibility and authenticity are inseparably bound together: "The self comes into its own as an I when faced with the phenomenon of death, and it comes into its own in the sphere of the 'I can' (possibility). It *does* come into its own; so there is an actuality, a fulfillment about it. But it comes into its own in the anticipation of the possibility that is most its own, the possibility of 'my-death.'" Scharlemann's answer to his own question now is clear: "What is the nature of the combination of the fulfillment [of the self] and the possibility [of death]"? *I* become *my* authentic self in and through *my* being toward the possibility of *my* death. This authenticity is the fulfillment of the self.[3]

Death, however, cannot be located on the axis that runs from possibility to actuality. To interpret death as the pure possibility that renders my actual authenticity possible is a humanistic gesture intended to domesticate death. But death is inhuman; it can never be humanized. Death is uncanny [*un-heim-lich*]; it can never be domesticated. "There is no doubt that we weaken Heidegger's thought when we interpret 'being-for-death' as the search for authenticity through death. We attribute to him the vision of a persevering humanism. To begin with, the term 'authenticity' does not do justice to *Eigentlichkeit,* which already suggests the ambiguities of the word *eigen* as they are to appear in *Ereignis*—the 'event' that cannot be understood in relation to 'being.'"[4] The event that cannot be understood in relation to "being" is, in a certain sense, impossible. "If death is the real, and if the real is impossible, then we are approaching the thought of the impossibility of death."[5] The real, whose silence Winquist evokes, is not the actual but is what cannot be actualized. The nonactualizable is the impossible. Impossibility is neither the simple negation of possibility nor the horizon of actuality. It is what interrupts the actuality of possibility and the possibility of actuality. The impossibility of death renders impossible the fulfillment of the self. Inasmuch as death is impossible, there can be no true or authentic relation to it. "Indeed, I elude it when I think I master it through a resolute acceptance, for then I turn away from what makes it the essentially inauthentic and the essentially inessential. From this point of view, death admits of no 'being *for* death'; it does not have the solidity that would sustain such a relation. It is that which happens to no one, the uncertainty and the indecision of what never happens. I cannot think about it seriously, for it is not serious. It is its own imposter; it is the disintegration, vacant debilitation—not the term but the interminable, not proper but featureless death, and not true death but, as Kafka says, 'the sneer of its capital error.'"[6]

The impossibility of death is disastrous. The disaster marks the death of God in which God becomes (the) Impossible. "Meaning of supplication. I express it thus, in the form of a prayer: O God our father, You who, in a night of despair, crucified Your son, who, in this night of carnage, as agony became *impossible*—to the point of distraction—became the *Impossible* Yourself and felt *impossibility* right to the point of horror—God of despair, give me that heart, Your heart, which fails, which exceeds all limits and tolerates no longer that You should be!"[7]

"What is it that links disaster and

apocalypse together as reciprocally exclusive?"

> But then what is someone doing who tells you: I tell you this, I have come to tell you this, there is not, there never has been, there never will be an apocalypse, the apocalypse deceives, disappoints? There is the apocalypse *without* apocalypse. . . . The *without*, the *sans* marks an internal and external catastrophe of the apocalypse, an overturning of sense [*sens*] that does not merge with the catastrophe announced or described in the apocalyptic writings without however being foreign to them. Here the catastrophe would perhaps be *of* the apocalypse itself, its *pli* and its end, a closure without end, an end without end.[8]

Apocalypse without apocalypse. End without end. Apocalypse and disaster are not precisely reciprocal or exclusive opposites.

They are coim-*pli*-cated in such a way that disaster "is" the failure of apocalypse. Inasmuch as this failure is not accidental but is
inevitable, disaster can be understood as the impossibility of
apocalypse.

Apocalypse is always (supposed to be) *now*—here and now.
This now involves a reversal (dialectical or otherwise) in which
what previously had been covered or concealed is uncovered or
revealed. *Apokalupsis*, revelation, derives from *apokaluptein*, to
uncover: *apo*, reversal + *kaluptein*, to cover. Revelation, disclosure, uncovering, stripping bare. "*Apokalupto*, I disclose, I uncover, I unveil, I reveal the thing that can be a part of the body, the
head or the eyes, a secret part, the genitals or whatever may be
hidden, a secret, the thing to be dissembled, a thing that does not
show itself or say itself, that perhaps signifies itself but cannot or
must not first be handed over to its self-evidence. *Apokekalummenoi logoi* are incident remarks. So it is a matter of the secret
and the *pudenda*."[9]

Apocalypse is always a matter of vision and visions. The Apocalypse is a vision about (coming) visions. "Behold, he is coming
with the clouds, and every eye will see him, every one who
pierced him; and all tribes of earth will wail on account of him.
Even so. Amen."[10] If, as Altizer maintains, history is an apocalyptic process that begins with "The Birth of Vision," it reaches closure in "a purely immediate speech."

> That speech is the real presence of resurrection, and its full enact-
> ment is the total presence of Apocalypse, a presence in which the
> dark and negative passion of God becomes immediately at hand.
> And it is immediately at hand insofar as it is actually spoken. Then
> the total silence and emptiness of an original abyss becomes imme-
> diately present chaos, but a chaos which is cosmos when it [is] res-
> urrected in language and word. The cosmos is the resurrected
> Christ, but a resurrected Christ who is inseparable and indistin-
> guishable from the crucified Christ, for now the Christ of glory *is*
> the Christ of passion. So it is that the body of this Christ can only
> be a dark and broken body, but it is a body which is present in all
> the immediacy of an unformed and primordial matter, as a totally
> fallen body now realizes itself in the pure immediacy of word.[11]

In apocalyptic vision, negation is negated. Absence becomes presence, silence becomes word, death becomes life. ". . . and 'Lff' is
all in all." The "color" of apocalypse is blue—International Klein

Blue. (Apocalypse: *ap*, away, *kel*, hollow, to cover, hide; blue: *bhel*, shine, blaze, burn, shimmer like a flame, *kel*, hollow, to cover, hide.)

But is speech ever immediate, presence ever total, absence ever absent; is Lff ever all in all? I think not. And in thinking not, I struggle to unthink apocalypse nonapocalyptically. I have come to tell you this, there is not, there never has been, there never will be an apocalypse, the apocalypse deceives, disappoints. Vision fails, always fails, for it presupposes a blind spot that renders it incomplete. Words fail, always fail, for they inscribe the absence they seek to erase. The failure of vision can be heard in the words of visionaries. Visions are prophetic—their tense is future, *always* future.

. . . he is coming with the clouds, and every eye *will* see him . . . The delay and deferral are not temporary but are interminable . . . endless.

The space of this delay, the time of this deferral is the spacing-timing of the disaster. The disaster neither occurs nor arrives. Rather, the disaster occurs as the nonoccurrence and nonarrival of the apocalypse. In this nonoccurrence and nonarrival *nothing happens.* "He does not believe in the disaster. One cannot believe in it, whether one lives or dies. Commensurate with it there is no faith, and at the same time a sort of disinterest, detached from the disaster. Night; white, sleepless night—such is the disaster: the night lacking darkness, but brightened by no light."[12] Night, white, sleepless night. A different wake, an other *Wake. Fin* again, and again, and again. *Fin* without end.

> *"Is nothingness beyond God, or*
>
> *is God beyond nothingness?"*

Within an apocalyptic economy, God is beyond nothingness; in the wake of the disaster, nothing is "beyond" God. Scharlemann correctly argues that "Altizer . . . aligns the concepts in such a way that God is beyond both being and nothing. Apocalypse is, therefore, the unveiling of God, and total presence is the presence of God." To locate God "beyond" nothing is to attempt to repress nothingness. This has always been one of the primary functions of the notion of God in Western religion and theology. The re-pressed, however, is not negated but repeatedly returns to disrupt and dislocate all efforts to domesticate nothing. The return of the repressed marks the nonsite of a nothing that is "beyond" God. This "beyond" is not transcendent but is an irreducible "exteriority" that is "within" all apparent presence and every purported self-presence. In different terms, the "beyond" of nothing is neither immanent nor transcendent. It "is" always elsewhere—nearer than presence, yet more distant than absence.

To claim that nothing is "beyond" God is not to declare God to be supreme but is to insist that God is dead. In this death, absence is not transformed into presence. The God whose death nothing implies is not merely the theistic God—the God who is conceived as a being, albeit the highest or greatest being. Nothing is beyond every vision of the divine in terms of being or its binary/polar/dialectical opposite, nonbeing. A being, being, and nonbeing remain caught in an ontological web that nothing unravels. To think this elusive nothing, the classical *via negativa* is no more adequate than the *via positiva*. Nothing can be thought, if at all, only by thinking *otherwise*.

> Fragmentation, the mark of a coherence all the firmer in that it has come undone in order to be reached, and reached not through a dispersed system, or through dispersion as a system, for fragmentation is the pulling to pieces (the tearing) of that which never has preexisted (really or ideally) as a whole, nor can it ever be reassembled in any future presence whatever. Fragmentation is the spacing of a temporalization that can only be grasped—fallaciously—as the absence of time.

> Fragments are written as unfinished separations. Their incompletion, their insufficiency, the disappointment at work in them, is their aimless drift, the indication that, neither unifiable nor consistent, they leave a certain spacing of marks—the marks with which thought (in decline and in declining itself) figures the furtive groupings that fictively open and close the absence of totality. Not that thought ever stops, definitively fascinated, at the absence; always carried on, by the watch, the ever-uninterrupted wake.[13]

"What is theology?"

"What is . . . ?" We are still within the domain of ontotheology. The task of thinking at the end of theology is, as I have suggested, to think what (onto)theology has left unthought. This unthought, which is, perhaps, unthinkable, provides no answer to any question of "What is . . . ?" To think after the end of theology (an end that never arrives) is to think otherwise by thinking a/theologically, which is not to say nontheologically. A/theological thinking does not "absorb" but displaces theological thinking. This displacement involves two closely related gestures. First, the theological tradition must be deconstructed. If the nothing that is to be thought is not simply "beyond" theology but is "within" it as an irreducible exteriority that can be neither negated nor absorbed, then thinking "begins" by soliciting the repressed in classical theological texts. In different terms, a/theology thinks the impossibility of theology. Second, a/theology cannot merely write *about* this impossibility but must write this impossibility itself. The writing of this impossibility is never complete but always fragmentary. The fragment inevitably disappoints, for it inscribes the failure of language. Language fails in what Edmond Jabès describes as "wounded words." The wound of words is a tear that cannot be mended—a tear that can never be wiped away. This tear is figured in Fontana's "Cuts." To write nothing is to inscribe the nonfigurable tear in and through the withdrawal of language.

To write the impossibility of theology is to rewrite the impossibility of death by rethinking the death of God radically. The death of God *is not* the birth of (the) all. The all is but a shadow of God—perhaps the darkest most ominous shadow in which the blue of Eden erupts in a flame that transforms apocalypse into holocaust. To unthink God, as well as the all, it is necessary to think the nothing that God and the all are constructed *not* to think. In the search for nothing, a/theology must look beyond overt religious activity and explicit theological concepts to broader forms of cultural expression. Art, literature, and psychoanalysis become indispensable resources for creative reflection. In this journey . . . from this journey, there is no return.

> Give me your hand:
> Now I'm going to tell you how I went into that inexpressiveness that was always my blind, secret quest. How I went into what exists between the number one and the number two, how I saw the mysterious, firey, line, how it is a surreptitious line. Between two musical notes there exists another note, between two facts there exists another fact, between two grains of sand, no matter how close together they are, there exists an interval of space, there

exists a sensing between sensing—in the interstices of primordial matter there is the mysterious, firey line that is the world's breathing, and the world's continual breathing is what we hear and call silence.

But—I return with the unsayable. The unsayable can be given to me only through the failure of my language. Only when the construct falters do I reach what it cannot accomplish.[14]

The death of God is a disaster. To think this disaster is to think the impossibility of theology by lingering with a negative that cannot be negated.

If I say: the divine has deserted the temples, that does not mean, as a ruse of dialectic is always ready to suggest, that the emptiness of the temples now offers us the divine. No: it means precisely and literally that the temples are deserted and that our experience of the divine is our experience of this desertion. It is no longer a question of meeting God in the desert: but of this—and *this* is the desert—: we do not encounter God, God has deserted all encounter.[15]

Desert . . . desertion . . . departure . . . dereliction . . . abandonment. A/theology mourns a passing that cannot be surpassed.

"What is a crypt?

No crypt presents itself. The grounds are so disposed as to disguise and to hide: something always a body in some way. But also to disguise the act of hiding and to hide the disguise: the crypt hides as it holds. . . . The crypt is thus not a natural place, but the striking history of an artifice, an *architecture*, an artifact: of a place *comprehended* within another but rigorously separated from it, isolated from general space by partitions, an enclosure, an enclave. So as to purloin *the thing* from the rest. Constructing a system of partitions, with their inner and outer surfaces, the cryptic enclave produces a cleft in space, in the assembled system of various places, in the architectonics of the open square within space, itself delimited by a generalized closure, in the *forum*. Within this forum, a place where the free circulation and exchange of objects and speeches can occur, the crypt constructs another, more inward

forum like a closed rostrum or speaker's box, a *safe*: sealed, and
thus internal to itself, a secret interior within the public square,
but, by the same token, outside it, external to the interior. Whatever one might write upon them, the crypt's parietal surfaces do
not simply separate an inner forum from an outer forum. The inner
forum is (a) safe, an outcast inside the inside."[16]

"My" words are graffiti scribbled on the crypt's parietal surfaces. What crypt? Whose crypt hollows out "my" words as if
from within? The crypt that renders language cryptic is the crypt
of the mother. Death is always in some sense the death of the
m-other—even when it is the death of the F/father or S/son.
Death repeats the nonevent that has always already taken place
and thus never actually takes place. The death of the mother arrives as an approaching withdrawal. Whether this withdrawal is
the mother's or the child's remains uncertain. What is certain is
that in withdrawing, death crypts. The crypt of death is the nonsite of a catastrophe or disaster that cannot be overcome in an
apocalypse.

The news of my [mother's] death came to me [two] weeks ago. It
was [Monday] morning, and I was in the kitchen. . . . Upstairs my
wife was still in bed, warm under the quilts, luxuriating in a few
extra [minutes] of sleep. Winter in the country: a world of silence,
wood smoke, whiteness. My mind was filled with thoughts about
the piece I had been writing the night before, and I was looking
ahead to the afternoon when I would be able to get back to work.
The phone rang. I knew instantly that there was trouble. No one
calls at [six] o'clock on a [Monday] morning unless it is to give
news that cannot wait. And news that cannot wait is always bad
news.
    I could not muster a single ennobling thought.
    Even before we packed our bags and set out on the [four] hour
drive to New Jersey, I knew that I would have to write about my
[mother]. I had no plan, had no precise idea of what this meant. I
cannot even remember making a decision about it. It was simply
there, a certainty, an obligation that began to impose itself on me
the moment I was given the news. I thought: my [mother] is
gone.[17]

Always (already) gone.

The Gospel According to Mark

They went into the tomb, where they saw a youth sitting on the right-hand side, wearing a white robe; and they were dumfounded. But he said to them, "Fear nothing; for you are looking for Jesus of Nazareth, who was crucified. He has been raised again; he is not here; look, there is the place where they laid him. But go and give his message to his disciples and Peter: 'He is going on before you into Galilee; there you will see him, as he told you.'" Then they went out and ran away from the tomb, beside themselves with terror. They said nothing to anybody, for they were afraid.[18]

They do not tell, they do not see. The message is not sent; the message does not arrive. In its place—t-error.

The silence of Jesus

apocalypse without apocalypse

. . . *dispatches* . . . addresses without message . . . without destination . . . without sender . . . without decidable addressee. . .

à Dieu

adieu

End without end. Dumfounded . . . struck dumb . . . unending strokes.

There is, of course, another ending to the story. The alternative ending erases the failure of vision and the absence of speech. "Fear nothing . . ." Words (of comfort or discomfort) spoken in the emptiness of a crypt. But even when erased, the end without end always leaves a trace. The gospel according to Mark "ends" with the silence of three women. "They say nothing . . ." In the wake of death, there is nothing left to say. Always nothing left to say. But how to say it? To say it again? And again, and again? Without end?

* * * * *

NOTES

1. Roland Barthes, *Roland Barthes,* trans. R. Howard (New York: Hill and Wang, 1977), p. 142.
2. Paul Auster, *The Invention of Solitude* (New York: Penguin Books, 1988), p. 5.
3. To Scharlemann's question "Can an escape *from* the 'I'-ness of the I be made?" I would "respond" with another question: "Can an escape *to* the 'I'-ness of the I be made?" Criticizing Winquist's analysis of Tillich, Scharlemann argues that there is no "way in which one can escape from being rooted in a singular, unexchangeable here-now that is indicated by the word 'I.'" However, in the ever-approaching shadow of death, the here-now is precisely what is not here or now. The I masks the here-now that is always already missing.
4. Blanchot, *The Writing of the Disaster,* p. 117.
5. Ibid., p. 121.
6. Blanchot, *The Space of Literature,* p. 155.
7. Georges Bataille, *Inner Experience,* trans. L. Boldt (New York: State Univ. of New York Press, 1988), p. 35.
8. Derrida, "Of an Apocalyptic Tone Recently Adopted in Philosophy," pp. 94–95.
9. Ibid., p. 64.
10. The Revelation of John, 1:7.
11. Altizer, *History as Apocalypse,* p. 254.
12. Blanchot, *The Writing of the Disaster,* p. 2.
13. Ibid., pp. 60, 58.
14. Clarice Lispector, *The Passion according to G. H.,* trans. R. W. Sousa (Minneapolis: Univ. of Minnesota Press, 1988), pp. 90, 170.
15. Jean-Luc Nancy, "Of Divine Places," *Paragraph* 7 (1986):43.
16. Jacques Derrida, "Foreword: *Fors:* The Anglish Words of Nicolas Abraham and Maria Torok," trans. B. Johnson, *The Wolf Man's Magic Word: A Cryptonymy,* trans. N. Rand (Minneapolis: Univ. of Minnesota Press, 1986), p. xiv.
17. Paul Auster, *The Invention of Solitude,* pp. 5–6. This passage is about the death of Auster's father. In a remarkable essay entitled "*Le* Christ mort, *de* Holbein,*" Julia Kristeva implicitly suggests a connection between the separation from the mother, the death of Christ, and writing: "The death of Christ offers an imaginary support to the irrepresentable catastrophic dread proper to melancholics. We know well that the so-called 'depressive' phase is essential for the entrance of the infant into the order of symbols and linguistic signs. This depression—sadness of separation as the condition for the representation of all things absent—returns and accompanies our symbolic activity when it is not exaltation but its reverse that it recovers. A suspension of meaning, a night without hope, the eclipse of perspectives and even of life, then rekindling in memory the remembrance of traumatic separations and plunging us into a state of abandonment. 'Father, why have you abandoned me?' Furthermore, clinical melancholy represents a true hell for man and still more, perhaps, for modern man who is convinced of the duty and ability to realize all the objects and values he desires. Christic dereliction offers an imaginary elaboration of this hell. It echoes for the subject his moments of insupportable loss of meaning and direction, loss of meaning and direction of life" (*Soleil Noir: Dépression et Mélancholie* [Paris: Gallimard, 1987], p. 144).
18. The Gospel according to Mark, 16:5–8.

CHARLES E. WINQUIST

INTERROGATIONS AND CLARIFICATIONS

ROBERT SCHARLEMANN's interrogation of the three essays by Altizer, Taylor, and myself is specific in its questioning of philosophical and theological formulations and is also generally an
inquiry into the possibilities and strategies for a theology at the
end of the ontotheological tradition or close of the metaphysical
epoch in the thinking of being. What is clear is that characteristic
of the three essays, although there are diverse sources and distinguishable trajectories for each of the essays, is their social location in the secular culture that distinguishes them from church
theologies. Altizer through his radical readings and expansion of
the Christian canon and Taylor and myself by working outside of
the overtly religious expressions of culture have raised the questions and must be responsible to the implications of the questions
as to whether secular theologies are possible and, if so, are they
important within our individual and cultural lives?

This is an inquiry as to whether there is a theological exigency
in thinking that matters even if we do not stand within a hermeneutical circle of a confessional tradition. It is not a matter of
apologetically situating faith within the claims of culture but it
is, instead, an interrogation of culture for those dimensions of experience that cannot be thematized or articulated without theological reflection of its boundaries, limits, fissures, and incor-
rigibilities. A secular theology does not start with a theological
agenda but discovers that agenda as an achievement of its thinking. It is not as if one can choose to step inside or outside traditional theological circles and that the work of secular theology is
a strategy of the outside. "Here I stand" is as much the problem of
the secular theologian as it was of Luther. If one stands outside
of a confessional community this does not mean that one also
stands outside of the range of ultimate concern.

But we do have to speak and write from where we stand. The

coincidence of the end of the twentieth century with the cultural dismantling of the ontotheological tradition in Western thought means that theology cannot step into the twenty-first century by simply carrying over the ballast from the nineteenth-century achievements of this tradition. Perhaps, most importantly, as Scharlemann stated in his *Response*, "what is being rejected is the possibility of finding a first, an irreducible principle, upon which everything is based and from which everything can be derived." If this rejection is credible and compelling, then what is radically changed is the status of "foundational" concepts in the formation of discursive practices. This does not mean that we cannot speak of subjectivity, objectivity, ontology, or even God; but it does mean that these concepts have been defamiliarized when shifted into a differential frame that is other than the ontotheological tradition. Many of the specific questions raised by Scharlemann will have to be adjudicated in relationship to this difference. In particular, we cannot begin by granting special privilege to discursive formations that reside outside of the specific text production of our inquiry and are not subject to the genealogical analysis that can come by reflecting the text back on itself.

The death of God, the closure of the book, the end of history, and the dismantling of a centered and unified subject are not desiderata of postmodern thought but are the problematic of this thinking. We cannot will away the historical and cultural witness of our time although we can always challenge the adequacy of interpretive formulations of where we stand. Scharlemann certainly does not deny the importance or the force of this problematic in his response to the three essays, but he does challenge, in response to Taylor and myself, the overvaluation of the phenomenon of self-dispersal in the reading of the postmodern condition.

Has too much importance been assigned to the loss of the unified subject in Taylor's a/theology or in my attempts to force metonymical strategies on theological discourse? Certainly, if it can be otherwise. What is at stake in this question is whether there is an epistemological framework that can both authenticate itself and be used to restore or rehabilitate the speculative thinking of the ontotheological tradition. It is in this sense that Scharlemann is correct to note that I reject or, I would prefer to say, that I am suspicious of Ricoeur's metaphorical approach and its relationship to notions of analogy in a heuristic restoration of

speculative discourse. It appears to me that a definition of interpretation that functions at the intersection of metaphorical and
speculative domains is constitutive of a subjectivity that privileges the speculative and all of its entailments including the containment of the semantic shock of metaphorical difference in the
production of discourse. My emphasis on metonymical formulations is a strategy of hesitation before the aporia of the general
metaphoricity of all language usage and not a denial of the extension of the concept of metaphor to discourse itself.

That is, my strategy is an expression of philosophical and theological minimalism that in the wake of a hermeneutics of suspicion is not able to recognize in certain fundamental philosophical
concepts anything other than the force of desire. Scharlemann is
correct in saying that part of what I appropriate from Lacan is the
"bar" between the symbolic and the real and that in my thinking
"the real is a heterological element in the symbolic." This would
also mean, as he suggests, that "symbols represent a desire of the
real" and "they do not provide a description of the real."

In this formulation, the question that I have raised is whether
figurations such as the real which are not assimilable into description function metaphorically or metonymically. If they function metonymically, it would be not credible to claim a primary
intuition, perception, or secondary cognition of reality or subjectivity that is not mediated by language and constituted in discourse. The veil of discourse is not lifted revealing the other of
language but is a more complex expression of the otherness in
language. This argument is a variation on and attempt to give expression to Derrida's theme that there is no transcendental signified. In particular, there is no transcendental subjectivity but
only transcendental interrogations of discursive practices.

Scharlemann questions whether I erase the distinction between
the subject who is the author of a text and the subject who is reading the text. The force of this question resides in his claim that "I
have an access to my own interiority . . . which I do not have to
the interiority of someone else." That I cannot make his claim in
any straightforward way erases the distinction between these two
subjectivities. Without a transcendental subjectivity to explain
the unity of apperception, the unity of the I who is speaking,
thinking, or now writing is a textual unity. The access to my interiority does not in my experience seem to be more than an extensive familiarity with those texts with which I have identified the

pronoun "I." It is precisely when I am not able to textualize disparate forces that I think an alternative text of losing myself in order to preserve the "I" of the text at all.

To be sure, the extensive familiarity that I have with the texts that "I" author in formal discourse or in informal reveries gives a different value to the subjectivity constituted in this complex of texts in contrast to texts that I read. But the separation between writing and reading is not clear and in some reading and listening practices, such as psychoanalysis, the transference and sometimes confusions of subjectivity are part of the dynamic of the practice. The unity of apperception is an achievement of discursive practices that accompanies the material aggregate of the body in its locations, and this aggregate is not itself explained by or dependent upon transcendental subjectivity. It was to give some account of the priority of the body over transcendental subjectivity that I advocated a return to the Freudian unconscious through Lacan.

I apparently have a different reading than Scharlemann of Lacan's claim that the unconscious is structured like a language. I do not think that Lacan understands the unconscious to be a subjectivity but that the unconscious represents an order of the non-realized and that to the extent that it is known it will be known symptomatically through fissures, gaps, paradoxes, and incongruities in the structurations of language. The unconscious is a trope within Freud's and Lacan's discourse that functions discursively not unlike the real in contributing to the incompleteness and undecidability of self-awareness.

What is shifted in the placement of these unassimilable metonymical tropes within a theoretical discourse is the valuation of the other concepts within the discourse. Concepts have their meaning as referenced in the differential play of signifiers and are implicated in the ambiguity of the general tropics of the discourse. I want to suggest that this applies to the formulation of ontological categories or structures as much as it does to other ideas.

Scharlemann's discussion of subject and object and self and world as epistemological and ontological designations that can claim a universality is indeed a challenge to my discussion of heterological infrastructures to subjectivities, but I think that it is an argument that can be folded into my position without a significant loss of intelligibility although it would then have a different valuation for the development of theological discourse.

I am not arguing that one cannot make a distinction between subjects and objects but whether this is necessarily an ontological distinction—is it possible that the distinction is more clearly an expression of the predicative structure of grammar in the language conventions with which we are familiar?

Scharlemann says that "if I were to contend that the ontological question [Why is there anything at all?], not in its formal structure but as a question actually asked, does not imply a subject and an object, the test is whether I can actually make such a denial without implying the subject-object structure. Does my denial imply a structure having the elements of *someone* making the denial and *something* being denied?" He then says of this retorsive argumentation: "It says only that the ontological structure is inescapable"

If the question were not an ontological question but something much more banal, such as Why is the wagon red?—would we not be able to make the same argument about the subject-object structure? Would we also suggest that there is something about the structure of wagon painting that is inescapable, or would we say that there is something about the subject-object structure in our conventional use of the language of interrogation that is inescapable? When an argument is framed in the ontotheological tradition it will confirm the inescapableness of ontology. This is a variation of my suggestion in the essay of what we also witness in the formulation of Tillich's formal criteria for theology. When the frame of the ontotheological tradition is looked at from the outside it implicates the inside of discourse in the language of ontology. And if it is looked at from the inside, ontology is then experienced as the ground of the discourse. In both cases it is looking through the frame darkly and not seeing it as a frame that implicates ontology in the discourse in a privileged way.

My suggestion that we approach the issue of multiple subjectivities through heterological rather than ontological structures is an attempt to interrogate the constitution of subjectivities in textual productions that are related to the interaction of diverse and heterogeneous forces. Subjectivity manifests itself in specific locations as the variable product of external multiplicities. It is the interrogation that asks what are the conditions of these possibilities that goes *below* the manifest expressions of subjectivity, and this is why I refer to structures in the folding of discourse as heterological infrastructures. The infrastructural designation is a way of characterizing a mode of interrogation rather than being

the description of a metadiscursive realm. Whatever else heterological infrastructures may be, they themselves are known only
as specific folds in discursive formations.

I will not dispute that there are structures or rules for the formation of all discursive practices, and this is why we can always
transcendentally interrogate a discursive practice of which the interrogation is itself a textual production. But I do not know how
we can move from the specificity of these interrogations to the
general application or universalization of specific structures except to index regularities when they are noticed. It seems that
what I have done is to generalize an exigency of interrogation
rather make any claim about the status of the heterological infrastructures. Heterological infrastructures would be ontological
if one could make a claim for the universality of ontological
structures. If, on the other hand, ontological structures are the
production of a specific inquiry or discursive fold, then we could
claim that ontological structures are a specific manifestation of
these heterological infrastructures. The second of these claims is
a much more minimal affirmation that reads against the grain of
ontological totalization. That is, being would itself become an
unassimilable trope within the formations of philosophical or
theological discourse from this perspective. I have tried to suggest
that this is how "being" has sometimes functioned in the Western
ontotheological tradition in the elaboration of various analogical,
metaphorical, or symbolic strategies.

I have tried to suggest that this is how "God" has sometimes
functioned in theological textual practices. Does it make a difference, or matter, if metonymical strategies are consciously developed as a part of theological agendas? As I have already suggested,
the placing of extreme formulations or unassimilable tropes into
a discourse shifts the valuation and status of other concepts. The
metonymical strategy is in a part a valuing of the general metaphoricity of language functions and a deliteralization of theological discourse. There is a freedom in this strategy to entertain the
fullness, richness, and diversity of traditional theological thinking as well as experiment with new formulations because of this
strategy taking theology outside of the boundedness of any particular frame that could restrict the range of its inquiry.

Most importantly, if the real is a heterological element within
the symbolic realm, metonymical pressure can intensify and
transform the ordinariness of a discourse by implicating it in the
desire for real. Whether formulations such as "God created" are

unassimilable tropes would have to be determined in the specificity of the circumstances of a particular discursive practice. Dead metaphors cannot be enlisted into the service of a metonymical strategy because they are assimilable and place no new pressure on the discourse. It is when demands are made on textual and intertextual referencing which cannot be met that there is an incompleteness and undecidability to the text that references what is other than itself.

All that is contained within the differential play of textual referencing is then implicated in that incompleteness. It is in this sense that the defamiliarization of a metonymical strategy is an intensification of a discourse that itself draws us closer to the human enigma, the meaning of its otherness, and the meaning of the other.

John

4-6-93

INDEX